Mina

WHO'S BURIED WHERE?

Compiled by Fred Delaney
Updated & corrected by Ian Godfrey

**ABSON
BOOKS
LONDON**

5 Sidney Square, London, E1 2EY
www.absonbooks.co.uk
e-mail absonbooks@aol.com

FRONT COVER:
Mary Queen of Scots Tomb **WA**
© Dean & Chapter of Westminister 2010

ISBN 978 0902920 859

Revised and updated 2010
Revised and reprinted 2013

CONTENTS

PREFACE

Some years ago I discovered this invaluable booklet by Fred Delaney but was disappointed to find, however, a number of errors. Over the years these have been corrected and additions made – this is the latest edition.

To the best of my knowledge all the information included here is authenticated from many sources, including Westminster Abbey's 'Official Guide', the 'Dictionary of National Biography', 'City of London Encyclopedia', Pevsner's The Buildings of England series, plus many visits to the places concerned.

I have attempted to keep this booklet as Fred Delaney intended and it is still, primarily, his work but with corrections and additions in his style.

My thanks go to all who have assisted over the years, including Stephen Whitwell CBE, Richard Mortimer and the Abbey Library staff, Pamela Carrington, Canon Anthony Harvey, and above all in the checking, Chris Birch. Cecil Hackett originally compiled information regarding medical entries. For this printing I also wish to acknowledge the input made by the staff of the Abbey bookshop.

Ian Godfrey 2010

ABBREVIATIONS

AC	ARCHBISHOP of CANTERBURY
B	BRASS
Bt	BARONET
c	APPROXIMATELY
C of E	CHURCH of ENGLAND
D	DESTROYED
G	GRAVESTONE
K	KILLED IN BATTLE
M	MURDERED
MEM	MEMORIAL
MON	MONUMENT
PM	PRIME MINISTER
R	REIGNED
RC	ROMAN CATHOLIC
T	TOMB (above ground structure)
WA	WESTMINSTER ABBEY
X	EXECUTED
YD	CHURCHYARD

ROYAL FAMILIES

ADELAIDE of SAXE-MEININGEN: 1792-1849
Queen, wife of William IV

St George's, Windsor

ADELA of LOUVAIN: c1104-1151
Queen, 2nd wife of Henry 1
(also called Adeliza and Adelia)

Convent of Afflighem
(Flanders, Belgium) where she died

ALBERT of SAXE-COBURG-GOTHA: 1819-1861
Prince Consort, husband of
Queen Victoria

Frogmore Mausoleum, in grounds
of Windsor Castle – open to the
public on Wednesday nearest
May 24th, Queen Victoria's
birthday

ALEXANDRA of DENMARK: 1844-1925
Queen, wife of Edward VII

St. George's, Windsor T

ALFONSO: 3rd son of Edward I 1273-1284

WA Confessor's chapel site
unknown; heart in Blackfriars,
London D

ALFRED THE GREAT: 849-899 (R 871-899)
and QUEEN ALSWITHA

Originally buried at Old Minster,
Winchester. Remains removed by
William the Conqueror to the New
Minster but bones dispersed at
the Reformation

ANNE, QUEEN: 1665-1714 (R 1702-1711)
Wife of George of Denmark

WA Henry VII Chapel south aisle

Mother of 17 children

WA 16 buried in Henry VII Chapel,
Stuart vault
1 buried St George's, Windsor,
Henry VIII vault

ANNE of BOHEMIA: 1366-1394
Queen, 1st wife of Richard II

WA Confessor's Chapel T

ANNE BOLEYN: 1507-1536 X
Queen, 2nd wife of Henry VIII

St. Peter-ad-Vincula, Tower of
London; heart possibly in
Erwarton church, Suffolk

ANNE of CLEVES: 1516-1557
Queen, 4th wife of Henry VIII

WA South side of Sanctuary;
became RC and buried by order
of Mary I T

ANNE of DENMARK: 1574-1619
Queen, wife of James 1

WA Henry VII Chapel G

ANNE HYDE: 1638-1671
1st wife of James Duke of York,
later James II

WA Henry VII Chapel South side,
Stuart Vault

ANNE MOWBRAY: 1472-1481
Duchess of York, wife of Richard,
younger of the princes in the Tower

WA Henry VII Chapel,
having been discovered in 1965
on site of Minories, London

ANNE NEVILL: 1456-1485
Queen, wife of Richard III

WA sanctuary, site unknown

ANTOINE PHILIPPE: 1775-1807
Duc de Montpensier, brother to
King Louis Philippe of France

WA Henry VII Chapel T
Died in exile in England during
Napoleonic Wars

ARTHUR & GUINEVERE: 6th century

Exhumed and reburied by
Edward I in 1278 at Glastonbury
Abbey. Site now in ruins GD

ARTHUR TUDOR: 1486-1502
Prince of Wales, elder brother of
Henry VIII;1st husband of
Catherine of Aragon

Worcester Cathedral T; heart in
St Laurence, Ludlow

ATHELSTAN, KING: 895-939 (R 925-939)
Half brother of Edward the Confessor's
great-grandfather

Malmesbury Abbey, Wilts,
medieval effigy T

AUGUSTA of SAXE-GOTHA: 1719-1772
Wife of Frederick, Prince of Wales,
mother of George III

WA Henry VII Chapel, nave

BEATRICE von FALKENBERG: 1253-1277
3rd wife of the Earl of Cornwall

Franciscan Church, Oxford D

BEAUFORT, see MARGARET

BEDFORD, JOHN, DUKE of: 1389-1435
Brother of Henry V

Rouen Cathedral, France

BERENGARIA of NAVARRE: c1163-1235
Queen, wife of Richard I

Espans Abbey, France, converted
to barn in 1790; effigy moved to
St Julien's, Le Mans in 1820

BLANCHE of LANCASTER: 1345-1369
1st wife of John of Gaunt

Old St Paul's, London,
T erected 1374 D in 1666 fire

BOTHWELL,
EARL of see **HEPBURN**

BRANDON, Charles
see **SUFFOLK**

CANUTE, KING: c995-1035 (R 1016-1035)
King of Denmark, Norway and England

Winchester Cathedral, remains in a wood chest

CAROLINE of ANSBACH: 1683-1737
Queen, wife of George II

WA Henry VII Chapel, nave

CAROLINE of BRUNSWICK: 1768-1821
Wife of George IV

Brunswick, Germany

CATHERINE of ARAGON: 1485-1536
Queen, 1st wife of Henry VIII

Peterborough Cathedral, Northants. TD in Civil War

CATHERINE of BREGANZA: 1638-1705
Queen, wife of Charles II

St Vincente de Fora Monastery, Lisbon

CATHERINE HOWARD: 1522-1542 X
Queen, 5th wife of Henry VIII

St. Peter-ad-Vincula, Tower of London

CATHERINE PARR: 1512-1548
Queen, 6th and last wife of Henry VIII

Sudeley Castle, Glos, TD in Civil War; present tomb 1858

CATHERINE of VALOIS: 1401-1437
Queen, wife of Henry V,
sister of 2nd wife of Richard II

WA Buried in early Lady Chapel; on public view for 200 years, then in Buckingham vault, now in altar of Henry V Chantry Chapel

CECILY NEVILLE: 1415-1495
Duchess of York

Fotheringhay Church, Northants, Elizabethan T

CHARLEMAGNE: ? - 814
King of the Franks 768
Holy Roman Emperor 800-814

Aachen Cathedral, Germany, remains in gold chest

CHARLES I: 1600-1649 X (R 1625-1649)
Husband of Henrietta Maria

St George's, Windsor in Henry VIII vault

CHARLES II: 1630-1685 (R 1660-1685)
Husband of Catherine of Braganza

WA Henry VII Chapel south aisle

CHARLES V: 1500-1558
Holy Roman Emperor & Charles I of Spain, Nephew of Catherine of Aragon

The Escorial nr Madrid, Spain

CHARLES EDWARD STUART: 1720-1788
'The Young Pretender', son of 'The Old Pretender' and Maria Clementia Sobieska

St Peter's Rome, with father

CHARLOTTE of MECKLENBURG-STRELITZ: 1744-1818
Queen, wife of George III

St George's, Windsor

CONSTANCE of CASTILE: 1354-1394
2nd wife of John of Gaunt

Possibly Old St Paul's Cathedral
but more likely St Mary's,
Leicester

DARNLEY, LORD HENRY
see Henry Stuart

DAVID II of SCOTLAND: 1324-1371 (R 1329-1371)
Son of Robert Bruce, husband of
Joanna sister of Edward III

Holyrood Abbey, Edinburgh, TD at
Dissolution, remains reburied in
post-Reformation vault in
East end of South aisle

DIANA SPENCER: 1961-1997
Princess of Wales

Althorp Estate, Northants

EDGAR: c944-975
1st King of the English (R 973-975)
King of Mercia 959

Glastonbury

EDITH: ?-1075
Queen, wife of Edward the Confessor

WA Confessor's Chapel

EDMUND: 840-879
King of the East Angles,
martyr and saint

Bury St Edmunds, Suffolk, ruins

EDMUND II: c993-1016 (R 1016)
Known as 'Ironside'

Glastonbury

EDMUND: 1245-1296
Known as 'Crouchback', 2nd son of Henry III

WA North side of Sanctuary T

EDMUND of LANGLEY: 1341-1402
Duke of York, 5th son of Edward III

Kings Langley, Herts. T in church
removed from suppressed
monastery

EDMUND of RUTLAND: 1443-1460
Brother of Edward IV

Fotheringhay Church, Northants,
Elizabethan T

EDMUND TUDOR: 1430-1456
Father of Henry VII

1st in Greyfriars Church,
Carmarthen; in 1536
removed to St David's Cathedral,
Pembrokeshire

EDWARD the CONFESSOR: c1004-1066
(R 1042-1066) Saint

WA Confessor's Chapel T

EDWARD I: 1239-1307 (R 1272-1307)
Husband of Eleanor of Castile,
then Margaret of France

WA Confessor's Chapel T

Edward 1st four children

WA South Ambulatory,
South wall T

EDWARD II: 1284-1327 M (R 1307-1327)
Husband of Isobella of France

Gloucester Cathedral T, heart, Greyfriars, London D

EDWARD III: 1312-1377 (R 1327-1377)
Husband of Philippa of Hainault

WA Confessor's Chapel T

EDWARD IV: 1442-1483 (R 1461-1483)
Husband of Elizabeth Woodville

St George's, Windsor

EDWARD V: 1470-1483 M (R Apr – June 1483)
Prince in the Tower, son of Edward IV

WA possible remains interred in 1678 in Henry VII Chapel north aisle

EDWARD VI: 1537-1553 (R 1547-1553)
Son of Henry VIII & Jane Seymour

WA under the altar of Henry VII Chapel

EDWARD VII: 1841-1910 (R 1901-1910)
Husband of Alexandra of Denmark

St George's, Windsor T

EDWARD VIII: 1894-1972 (R Jan-Dec 1936)
Son of George V, Duke of Windsor, husband of Wallis Simpson

Frogmore Burial Ground, Windsor

EDWARD the BLACK PRINCE: 1330-1376
Eldest Son of Edward III

Canterbury Cathedral T

EDWARD the MARTYR: 961-978 M (R 975-978)
Half-brother of Ethelred the Unready, Saint

Originally Wareham, moved to Shaftesbury Abbey 981, discovered 1931, finally taken to the Church and Shrine of St Edward the Martyr, Brookwood Cemetery, London

EDWARD: 1453-1471 M
Prince of Wales, only son of Henry VI

Tewkesbury Abbey, Gloucestershire, 18th Century G

EDWARD: 1473-1484
Prince of Wales, son of Richard III

Sheriff Hutton Church, North Yorkshire

EDWARD: 1373-1415 K
2nd Duke of York, grandson of Edward III

Fortheringhay Church, Northants, killed at Agincourt, Elizabethan MON

ELEANOR of AQUITAINE: 1122-1204
Queen, wife of Henry II

Fontevrault Abbey, France T

ELEANOR de BOHUN: ?-1399
Wife of Thomas Woodstock

WA Chapel of St Edmund T, B

ELEANOR of CASTILE: c1244-1290
1st wife of Edward I

WA Confessor's Chapel T, heart in Blackfriars, London D, entrails Lincoln Cathedral TD.
Victorian reconstruction

ELEANOR of PROVENCE: c1217-1291
Queen, wife of Henry III

Amesbury Convent, Wilts D. Heart, Franciscan Church, London D

ELIZABETH I: 1533-1603 (R 1558-1603)
Daughter of Henry VIII & Anne Boleyn

WA Henry VII Chapel, North aisle

ELIZABETH of BOHEMIA: 1596-1662
'The Winter Queen', eldest daughter of James I, mother of Prince Rupert.

WA Henry VII Chapel, South aisle, Stuart vault.

ELIZABETH BOWES-LYON: 1900-2002
Queen, wife of George VI

St George's Chapel, Windsor Castle G

ELIZABETH of LANCASTER: 1363-1425
Daughter of John of Gaunt

Burford, Shropshire T

ELIZABETH de la POLE: 1444-1503
Sister of Edward IV and Richard III

St Andrew's Church, Wingfield, Suffolk

ELIZABETH WOODVILLE: 1437-1492
Queen, wife of Edward VI

St George's, Windsor, with husband TD

ELIZABETH OF YORK: 1465-1503
Queen, wife of Henry VII

WA Henry VII Chapel T

ETHELRED II: c968-1016 M
(R 979-1013 and 1014-1016)
'The Unready', father of Edward the Confessor

Old St Paul's Cathedral, D by fire 1087

ETHELWULF: 839-858
King of the East Saxons, father of Alfred the Great

Winchester Cathedral

EUGENIE: 1826-1920
Empress of the French, wife of Napoleon III

Farnborough Abbey, Hants T

FERDINAND of ARAGON: 1452-1516
Father of Catherine of Aragon

Granada Cathedral, Spain T

FRANCIS I of FRANCE: 1494-1547

St Denis, Paris T

FRANCIS II of FRANCE: 1544-1560
1st husband of Mary Queen of Scots

St Denis, Paris T

FREDERICK, DUKE of SUSSEX: 1773-1843
6th son of George III

Kensal Green Cemetery London

GEOFFREY PLANTAGENET: 1158-1186
3rd Son of Henry II

Notre Dame, Paris

GEORGE I: 1660-1727 (R 1714-1727)
Husband of Sophia Dorothea of Celle

Originally, Hanover, Germany,
moved to Herrenhausen 1957

GEORGE II: 1683-1760 (R 1727-1760)
Husband of Caroline of Ansbach, 1st son of George I

WA Henry VII Chapel nave

GEORGE III: 1738-1820 (R 1760-1820)
Husband of Charlotte of Mecklenburg-Strelitz
1st son of Frederick, Prince of Wales

St George's, Windsor

GEORGE IV: 1762-1830 (R 1820-1830)
Husband of Caroline of Brunswick
1st son of George III

St George's, Windsor

GEORGE V: 1865-1936 (R 1910-1936)
Husband of Mary of Teck
2nd son of Edward VII

St George's, Windsor T

GEORGE VI: 1895-1952 (R 1936-1952)
Husband of Elizabeth-Bowes Lyon
2nd son of George V

St George's, Windsor G

GEORGE, DUKE of CLARENCE: 1449-1479 X
Brother of Edward IV and Richard III

Tewkesbury Abbey, Glos.
Remains in glass case on platform,
in vault, to protect it from water.
Vault not visible

GEORGE of DENMARK: 1653-1708
Husband of Queen Anne

WA Henry VII Chapel South aisle

HAROLD 1: c1016-1040 (R 1035-1040)
'Harefoot', 2nd Son of Canute

WA originally, then to church on
site of present St Clement Danes.
Disinterred and finally flung into
a marsh

HAROLD II: 1022-1066 K (R Jan-Oct 1066)
Son of Godwin, killed at Hastings

Beneath High Altar of Waltham
Abbey, Essex

HENRIETTA MARIA: 1609-1669
Queen wife of Charles I,
daughter of Henry IV of France

St Denis, Paris. Heart in Convent
of Visitation, Chaillot

HENRY I: 1068-1135 (R1100-1135)
Husband of Mathilda of Scotland and
Adele of Louvain

Reading Abbey, Berks D. Brain,
eyes, internal organs in Rouen,
France

HENRY II: 1133-1189 (R 1154-1189)
Husband of Eleanor of Aquitaine

Fontevrault Abbey, France T

HENRY III: 1207-1272 (R 1216-1272)
Husband of Eleanor of Provence

WA Confessor's Chapel in the upper section of T. Heart originally in Fontevrault Abbey, France. Escaped destruction at Revolution and now with Ursuline Nuns, Edinburgh

Children of HENRY III:
Princess Katherine aged 5 and 4 others

WA South wall of South Ambulatory T

HENRY IV: 1367-1413 (R 1399-1413)
Husband of Mary de Bohun and Joanna of Navarre

Canterbury Cathedral, with 2nd wife T

HENRY V: 1387-1422
Husband of Catherine of Valois

WA entrails in Church of St Maur-des-Fosses, France. D; body dismembered, boiled, bones and flesh returned to England for burial under his Chantry Chapel

HENRY VI: 1421-1471 M (R 1422-1461 and 1470-1471)
Husband of Margaret of Anjou

Originally Chertsey Abbey, moved to St George's, Windsor.

HENRY VII: 1457-1509 (R 1485-1509)
Husband of Elizabeth of York

WA Henry VII Chapel T

HENRY VIII: 1491-1547 (R 1509-1547)
Husband of Catherine of Aragon, Anne Boleyn, Jane Seymour, Anne of Cleves, Catherine Howard, Catherine Parr

St George's, Windsor As requested in his will, buried with his third wife Jane Seymour. Modern G

HENRY: 1267-1274
2nd son of Edward 1 and Eleanor of Castile

WA probably in T South ambulatory

HENRY of ALMAYNE: 1235-1271 M
Son of Richard, Earl of Cornwall

Hayles Abbey, Glos D. Heart Confessor's Chapel WA

HENRY FITZROY: 1519-1536
Duke of Richmond, illegitimate son of Henry VIII by Bessie Bount

St Michael's Church, Fraulingham, Suffolk

HENRY FREDERICK: 1594-1612
Prince of Wales, 1st Son of James I

WA Henry VII Chapel South aisle

HENRY STUART: 1545-1567
Lord Darnley, 2nd husband of Mary Queen of Scots

Holyrood Abbey, Edinburgh

HENRY TUDOR: 1511-1511
1st son of Henry VIII and Catherine of Aragon

WA near entrance to Henry VII Chapel, site unknown

HEPBURN, JAMES: 1536-1578
Earl of Bothwell, 3rd husband of
Mary Queen of Scots

Faarevejle Church, Denmark;
mummified corpse on view in
crypt until 1978 then buried

HUMPHREY: 1390-1447
Duke of Gloucester, brother of Henry V

St Albans Abbey, remains of T

ISABELLA of ANGOULEME: 1188-1246
Queen, 2nd wife of King John

Fontevrault Abbey, France T

ISABELLA QUEEN of CASTILE: 1451-1504
Mother of Catherine of Aragon

Granada Cathedral, Spain T

ISABELLA of FRANCE: c1295-1358
Wife of Edward II

Greyfriars, London D. Heart may
be at Castle Rising, Norfolk

ISABELLA of FRANCE: 1389-1409
Queen, 2nd wife of Richard II

Blois, France; moved to church
of Celestines, Paris

ISABELLA of PEMBROOKE: 1200-1240
1st wife of Richard, Earl of Cornwall

Beaulieu Abbey, Hants, grave slab

JAMES I of ENGLAND: 1566-1625 (R 1603-1625)
& JAMES VI of SCOTLAND: (R 1567-1625)
Husband of Anne of Denmark, son of
Mary Queen of Scots

WA in vault in Henry VII Chapel

JAMES II of ENGLAND: 1633-1701 (R 1685-1688)
& JAMES VII of SCOTLAND
Husband of Anne Hyde and Mary Modena

Some entrails in Church of
St Germain-en-Laye, France and
English College at St Omer; brains
in Scots college Paris, heart at
Chaillot; remains in Church of
English Benedictine monks, Paris,
despoiled at French Revolution

JAMES FITZJAMES: 1670-1734
Duke of Berwick, illegitimate son of James II

Church of English Benedictine
Monks, Paris

JAMES I of SCOTLAND: 1394-1437 M (R 1406-1437)
Husband of Joan Beaufort, 3rd son of Robert III

Carthusian Church in Perth D;
heart in Jerulsalem but returned
to the Carthusians in 1443

JAMES II of SCOTLAND: 1430-1460 (R 1437-1460)
Husband of Mary of Gueldres, 2nd son of James I

Holyrood Abbey, Edinburgh, TD at
Dissolution

JAMES III of SCOTLAND: 1451-1488 (R 1460-1488)
Husband of Margaret of Denmark,
1st son of James II

Cambuskenneth Abbey,
Stirlingshire

JAMES IV of SCOTLAND: 1473-1513 K (R 1488-1513)
Husband of Margaret Tudor, 1st son of James III

Killed at Flodden; body in Sheen
monastery, London,removed and
buried in charnel house of
St Michael's in the City 1610 D

JAMES V of SCOTLAND: 1512-1542 (R 1513-1542)
Husband of Mary of Guise, 3rd son of James IV,
father of Mary Queen of Scots

Holyrood Abbey, Edinburgh

JAMES VI of SCOTLAND
See JAMES I of ENGLAND

JAMES FRANCIS EDWARD STUART: 1688-1766
'The Old Pretender', 6th son of James II

St Peter's Rome, T erected 1819

JANE GREY, Lady: 1537-1554 X
Grand-daughter of Henry VIII's sister Mary,
reigned for 9 days

St Peter-ad-Vincula, Tower of
London

JANE SEYMOUR: c1509-1537
Queen, 3rd wife of Henry VIII, mother of Edward VI

St George's, Windsor with
Henry VIII in vault

JOAN: 1165-1199
3rd daughter of Henry II

Fontevrault Abbey, France

JOAN: 1210-1238
Queen of Scotland, wife of Alexander II, eldest
daughter of John, sister of Henry III

Tarrant Crawford, Dorset tomb lid

JOAN of ACRE: 1272-1307
4th daughter of Edward I

Clare Priory, Suffolk, ruins

JOAN HOLLAND: 1328-1385
'The Fair Maid of Kent', wife of The Black Prince,
Lincs, mother of Richard II

Greyfriars Monastery Stamford,
Lincs, with 3rd husband D

JOAN OF NAVARRE: c1370-1437
Queen, 2nd wife of Henry IV

Canterbury Cathedral with
Henry IV T

JOHN: 1167-1216 (R 1199-1216)
Husband of Isabella of Gloucester &
Isabella of Angoulême, 5th son of Henry II

Worcester Cathedral T, heart at
Croxton Abbey, Lincs D

JOHN: 1266-1271
1st son of Edward I

WA South Ambulatory T

JOHN of ELTHAM: 1316-1336
Earl of Cornwall, 2nd son of Edward II

WA Chapel of St Edmund T

JOHN of GAUNT: 1340-1399
Duke of Lancaster, husband of Blanche
of Lancaster, Constance of Castile,
Katherine Swynford, 4th son of Edward III

Old St Paul's Cathedral, London,
with Blanche and Constance:
D in 1666

KATHERINE SWYNFORD: 1350-1403
3rd wife of John of Gaunt

Lincoln Cathedral Choir T

LOUIS XI of FRANCE: 1423-1483

Basilica of North Dame, Clery, near Orleans, France T

LOUIS XVI of FRANCE: 1754-1793 X
Husband of Marie Antoinette

St Denis, Paris G

MACBETH: ?-1057

Isle of Iona, Scotland with 47 other Scottish kings

MARGARET of ANJOU: 1429-1482
Queen, wife of Henry VI

Angers Cathedral, France, in parent's vault

MARGARET BEAUFORT: 1443-1509
Mother of Henry VII

WA Henry VII Chapel South aisle T

MARGARET of FRANCE: 1279-1317
Queen, 2nd wife of Edward I

Greyfriars, London D; in Elizabeth's reign the mayor of London sold 10 tombs of which Margaret's was one

MARGARET: 1930-2002
Princess, Countess of Snowdon, younger daughter of George VI, sister of Queen Elizabeth II

St George's Chapel, Windsor G

MARGARET, Saint: c1045-1093
Wife of Malcolm II of Scotland, daughter of Edward Atheling

Tynemouth then Dunfermline Abbey; disinterred at Reformation. Head in silver casket at Scotch college, Douai, France, seen 1785

MARGARET TUDOR: 1489-1541
Wife of James IV of Scotland, sister of Henry VIII

Carthusian Church, Perth, with James I of Scotland D

MARIA CLEMENTINA SOBIESKA: 1702-1735
Wife of 'The Old Pretender'

St Peter's, Rome, heart in Church of Santi Apostoli, Rome

MARIE ANTOINETTE: 1755-1793 X
Wife of Louis XVI

St Denis, Paris G

MARY I: 1516-1558 (R 1553-1558)
Mary Tudor, known as 'Bloody Mary', wife of Philip II of Spain, daughter of Henry VIII and Catherine of Aragon

WA Henry VII Chapel, North aisle, with Elizabeth; heart in lead box

MARY II: 1662-1694 (R 1688-1694)
Wife of William of Orange, 1st daughter of James II

WA Henry VII Chapel South aisle

MARY: 1631-1660
1st Princess Royal, daughter of Charles I, mother of William III

WA Henry VII Chapel South aisle, Stuart vault

MARY de BOHUN: c1370-1394
1st wife of Henry IV

St Mary's Leicester, later removed to Holy Trinity Hospital Chapel, Leicester T

MARY of GUISE: 1515-1560
Wife of James V of Scotland, mother of Mary Queen of Scots

Rheims Cathedral, France

MARY of MODEA: 1658-1718
Queen, second wife of James II

Abbey of Chaillot, France D

MARY QUEEN of SCOTS: 1542-1587 X
Wife of Francis II of France, Lord Darnley & Lord Bothwell, daughter of James V, mother of James I and VI

WA originally buried in Peterborough Cathedral; removed by James I, in 1612, to WA Henry VII Chapel, South aisle

MARY of TECK: 1867-1953
Queen, wife of George V

St George's, Windsor T

MARY TUDOR: 1496-1533
Wife of Louis XII of France and Charles Brandon, Duke of Suffolk: sister of Henry VIII

Bury St Edmunds Abbey, Suffolk; at Dissolution in 1539 moved to St Mary's Church in Bury St Edmunds; gravestone near altar

MARY of YORK: 1466-1482
Daughter of Edward IV

St George's, Windsor

MATILDA (or MAUDE) of SCOTLAND: 1079-1118
Queen, wife of Henry I, daughter of Malcolm III and St Margaret

WA Confessor's Chapel; claimed also by Reading Abbey, Winchester Cathedral and Old St Paul's

MATILDA: 1102-1167
Empress wife of Henry V 'Holy Roman Emperor' then Geoffrey Plantagenet, Count of Anjou, daughter of Henry I

Abbey of Bec, France

MATHILDA of BOULOGNE: c1105-1152
Queen, wife of Steven

Faversham Abbey, Kent, D at Dissolution

MATILDA of FLANDERS: c1031-1083
Queen, wife of William I

Holy Trinity Church, Caen, France. TD in 1562 by Calvinists; bones reburied in casket under original stone slab which remains; examined in 1961, she was 50 inches tall

MONMOUTH, JAMES DUKE of: 1649-1685 X
illegitimate son of Charles II and Lucy Walter

St Peter-ad-VinCula, Tower of London

NAPOLEON I: 1769-1821
Emperor of the French

Originally St Helena, reinterred in Les Invalides, Paris, 1840

JAFFA: Napoleon's horse — Glassenbury Manor, Cranbrook, Kent, 38 years old

NAPOLEON III: 1808-1873
Emperor of the French, husband of
Empress Eugenie — Farnborough Abbey, Hants T

OFFA: ? – 1796 (R 757-796)
King of Mercia — Chapel on the Ouse nr Bedford

OSRIC: 7th CENTURY
Prince of Mercia — Gloucester Cathedral T

OWEN TUDOR: c1400 – 1461 X
2nd husband of Catherine of Valois,
great grandfather of Henry VIII — Greyfriars, Hereford D

PHILIP II of SPAIN: 1527-1598
Husband of Mary I — The Escorial, Spain T

PHILIPPA of HAINAULT: 1314-1369
Queen, wife of Edward III — WA Confessor's Chapel

POLE, MARGARET: 1473-1541 X
Countess of Salisbury, the last Plantagenet — St Peter-ad-Vincula, Tower of London

RICHARD I: 1157-1199 (R 1189-1199)
'Lionheart', husband of Berengaria,
2nd son of Henry II — Heart in Rouen Cathedral, moved to museum, viscera in Chalus, France, body in Fontevrault Abbey, France T

RICHARD II: 1367-1400 M (R 1377-1399)
Husband of Anne of Bohemia and Isabella
of France, son of Edward, the Black Prince — Kings Langley, Herts; moved by Henry V to WA Confessor's Chapter T

RICHARD III: 1452-1485 K (R 1483-1485)
Husband of Anne Nevill — Greyfriars Church, Leicester, D at Dissolution; bones thrown into River Soar; tablet near Bow Bridge Leicester

RICHARD PLANTAGENET: 15th Century
Illegitimate son of Richard III — Eastwell, Kent G

RICHARD EARL of CAMBRIDGE: c1376-1415 X
Father of Richard of York — French Protestant Church, Southampton

RICHARD EARL of CORNWALL: 1209-1272
King of the Romans, husband of Isabella, Sanchia
& Beatrice, brother of Henry III — Hayles Abbey, Glos, ruins; tablet marks grave. Heart in Franciscan Church, Oxford D

RICHARD DUKE of YORK: 1411-1460 X
Father of Edward IV — Fotheringhay Church, Northants, Elizabethan T

RICHARD DUKE of YORK: 1473-1483 M
Prince in the Tower

WA possible remains discovered in Tower in 1674 & interred 1678 in Henry VII Chapel, North aisle

ROBERT DUKE of NORMANDY: c1054-1134
1st son of William I

Gloucester Cathedral before High Altar, 13th century effigy

ROBERT BRUCE: 1274-1329 (R 1306-1329)
King of Scotland, husband of Isabella Mar, then Elizabeth de Burgh

Dunfermline Abbey, Fife; heart in Melrose Abbey, Roxburghshire, Scotland

RUPERT: 1619-1682
Prince, 3rd son of Elizabeth of Bohemia

WA Henry VII Chapel Stuart vault

SANCHIA of PROVENCE: c1225-1261
2nd wife of Richard Earl of Cornwall

Hayles Abbey, Glos; buried with the Earl

SOPHIA DOROTHEA of CELLE: 1666-1726
Wife of George I

Celle, Germany

STEPHEN: 1096-1154 (R 1135-1154)
Grandson of William the Conqueror & last Norman King of England

Faversham Abbey, Kent D

SUFFOLK, CHARLES BRANDON, DUKE OF: 1484-1545
2nd husband of Henry VIII's sister, Mary

St George's, Windsor

SUSSEX, FREDERICK DUKE OF: 1773-1843
6th son of George III

Kensal Green Cemetery, London

SWEYN: c986-1014 (R 1013-1014)

Roskilde Cathedral, Denmark

THOMAS of WOODSTOCK: 1355-1397
Duke of Gloucester, 7th son of Edward III

WA Confessor's Chapel, under floor in front of Edward III

VICTORIA: 1819-1901 (R 1837-1901)
Queen, wife of Albert of Saxe-Coburg-Gotha

Frogmore Mausoleum in grounds of Windsor Castle. Open to public on Wednesday nearest her birthday, 24th May

WALLIS, DUCHESS of WINDSOR: 1896-1986
Wife of Earl Winfield Spencer, Ernest Simpson & the Duke of Windsor, previously Edward VIII

Frogmore burial ground, Windsor

WILLIAM I: 1028-1087 (R1066-1087)
'The Conqueror', husband of Matilda

Caen, France; in 1562 Calvinists destroyed monument and scattered remains. One thigh bone remained; reburied under new monument which was destroyed by rioters 1733. Thigh bone today is perhaps under 19th century grave slab

WILLIAM II: 1056-1100 M (R 1087-1100)
'Rufus'

Winchester Cathedral

WILLIAM III: 1650-1702 (R 1688-1702)
'of Orange', husband of Mary II

WA Henry VII Chapel South aisle

WILLIAM IV: 1765-1837 (R 1830-1837)
Husband of Adelaide of Saxe-Meiningen

St George's Windsor

WILLIAM AUGUSTUS,
DUKE of CUMBERLAND: 1721-1765
3rd son of George II, 'Butcher of Culloden'

WA Henry VII Chapel, nave

WILLIAM of HATFIELD: 1336-1346
2nd son of Edward III

York Minster

FAMOUS PEOPLE

ABELARD, Peter: 1079-1142
Theologian (of Abelard & Heloise)

Père Lachaise Cemetery, Paris

ADAM, Robert: 1728-1792
Architect

WA Poets' Corner

ADDISON, Joseph: 1672-1719
Essayist

WA Henry VII Chapel North aisle.
MON Poets' Corner

AIRY, Sir George: 1801-1892
46 years Astronomer Royal

St Mary's, Playford, Suffolk, YD

ALARD, Admiral Gervase: 14th CENTURY
First Englishman to be called 'Admiral'

Winchelsea, East Sussex T

ALEXANDER, Mrs Cecil Frances: 1818-1895
Hymn writer, 'All Things Bright and Beautiful'

Londonderry City Cemetery

ALICE IN WONDERLAND
See **Liddell**

ALLENBY, Edmund: 1861-1936
1st Viscount Allenby

WA St George's Chapel

ALMA-TADEMA, Sir Lawrence: 1836-1912
(or Laurens) Artist

St Paul's Cathedral, London

ANDRE, Major John: 1751-1780 X
Hanged as a spy in American Revolutionary War

Originally buried at Tappan, NY,
USA, returned to the UK 1821.
WA nave

ANDREWES, Lancelot: 1555-1626
Bishop of Winchester. Helped prepare
Authorised Version of King James Bible

Southwark Cathedral T

ANSELM, Saint: 1033-1109 (AC 1093-1109)

Canterbury Cathedral T

ANSTEY, Christopher: 1724-1805
Author

St Swithin's, Bath, MEM WA
South Transept

ARNE, Dr Thomas: 1710-1778
Composer of 'Rule Britannia'

St Paul's, Convent Garden,
London

ARNOLD, General Benedict: 1741-1801
Sold plans of West Point defences to Major André. QV

St Mary's, Battersea, London

ARNOLD, Matthew: 1822-1888
Poet, son of Thomas

All Saints, Laleham, Middlesex, YD.
MEM and bust WA Poets' Corner

ARNOLD, Thomas: 1794-1842
Headmaster, Rugby School

Rugby Chapel, Warwicks.
Bust WA NW Tower

ARREHENIUS, Svante August: 1859-1927
Founder of physical chemistry

Uppsala, Sweden

ARTOIS, Count Robert III of France: 1287-1343
Friend of Edward III

Old St Paul's Cathedral, London, D

ARUNDEL, Earls of
See **Fitzalan** and **Howard**

ARUNDEL, Thomas: 1353-1414 (AC 1396-1414)
Crowned Henry IV

Canterbury Cathedral

ASCHAM, Roger: 1515-1568
Tutor to Elizabeth and Jane Grey

Holy Sepulchre, London

ASHBURNHAM, Sir John: 1603-1671
Loaned money to Charles I

St Peter, Ashburnham,
East Sussex T

ASHBURNHAM, William: ?-1679
Brother of John. Owner of Ashburnham
House, part of WA precincts

St Peter, Ashburnham,
East Sussex T

ASHCROFT, Dame Peggy: 1907-1991
Actress

Ashes scattered around Mulberry
Tree in Shakespeare's Garden,
Stratford-upon-Avon.
MEM WA Poets' Corner

ASHMOLE, Elias: 1617-1692
Founder Åshmolean Museum

St Mary's, Lambeth, London

ASHTON, Sir Frederick: 1904-1988
Ballet dancer & choreographer

St Mary, Yaxley, Suffolk, YD
MEM WA Poets' Corner

ASQUITH, Herbert: 1852-1928
1st Earl of Oxford & Asquith, PM 1908-1916

All Saints, Sutton Courtnay, Berks
YD. MEM WA North Transept

ATTLEE, Clement: 1883-1967
1st Earl Atlee, PM 1945-1951

WA Nave

AUDEN, WH (Wystan Hugh): 1907-1973
Poet

Kirchstetten, Austria. MEM WA
Poets' Corner

AUGUSTINE, Saint: ?-604
First AC 597-604

St Augustine's Abbey, Canterbury,
Kent

AUSTEN, Jane: 1775-1817
Novelist

Winchester Cathedral, MEM WA
Poets' Corner

BABBAGE, Charles: 1792-1871
Mathematician, first calculating machine.
Brain preserved in Lincoln's Inn

Kensal Green Cemetery, London

BABINGTON, Anthony: 1561-1586 X
Babington Plot

No record of burial

BACH, Johann Sebastian: 1685-1750
Composer

Thomas-Kirche, Leipzig, Germany

BACH, Johann Christian: 1735-1782
11th son of Johann Sebastian

St Pancras Old Church, London

BACON, Sir Francis: 1561-1626
Viscount St Albans, Lord Chancellor, philosopher

St Michael's, St Albans, Herts

BACON, John: 1740-1799
Sculptor of Pitt's monument WA
and Dr Johnson's in St Paul's

Whitefield's Tabernacle, London D

BACON, Sir Nicholas: 1509-1579
Elizabeth's Keeper of the Great Seal

Old St Paul's Cathedral, London
Damaged effigy in present
Cathedral crypt

BACON, Roger: c1214-1294
Franciscan philosopher

Oxford, site unknown

BADEN-POWELL, Robert: 1857-1941
1st Baron Baden-Powell, founder of
Boy Scout movement

Nyere, Kenya, MEM WA Nave

BADEN-POWELL, Lady Olave: 1889-1977
Wife of the above

Ashes with husband MEM WA
Nave

BAHA-ALLAH: 1817-1892
Divine Messenger of the Baha'i Faith

Acre, Israel

BAKEWELL, Robert: 1725-1795
'Greatest agricultural pioneer in the world'

Old Church, Dishley, Leics

BALDWIN, Stanley: 1867-1947
1st Earl Baldwin of Bewdley. Three times
PM: 1923-1924, 1924-1929 & 1935-1937

Worcester Cathedral G, MEM WA
Nave

BALFOUR, Arthur James: 1848-1930
1st Earl of Balfour, PM 1902-1905

Private family burial ground
Whittingehame Estate, near
Haddington, East Lothian

BALLIOL, John: ?-1269
Founder of Balliol College, Oxford

His heart buried Brabourne, Kent

BANKS, Sir Joseph: 1744-1820
Botanist, voyaged with Cook

St Leonard, Heston, Hounslow, Middlesex YD

BARBIROLLI, Sir John: 1899-1970
Conductor

St Mary's RC Cemetery, Kensal Green, London

BARLOW, William: ?-1568
Bishop of Chichester; one of 4 bishops (former RC) who consecrated Archbishop Parker (C of E) thus preserving the succession of Anglican bishops from those of the medieval church

Chichester Cathedral T

BARNARDISTON, Sir Samuel: 1620-1707
'First Roundhead'

SS Peter and Paul, Kedington, Suffolk

BARNADO, Dr Thomas: 1845-1905
Philanthropist & founder of homes for destitute children

Girls' village home, Barkingside, Redbridge, London

BARRETT, Edward: ?-1857
Father of Elizabeth Barrett Browning

St Michel, Ledbury, Hereford, M

BARRY, Sir Charles: 1795-1860
Architect, with Pugin, of Houses of Parliament

WA nave B

BARTON, Elizabeth: 1506-1534X
'Holy Maid of Kent'

Greyfriars Cemetery London D

BAYLIS, Lilian: 1874-1937
Founder of the Old Vic Theatre

East London Cemetery

BEATTY, Admiral David: 1871-1936
1st Earl Beatty

Last burial in St Paul's Cathedral, London

BEAUCHAMP, Richard: 1382-1439
Earl of Warwick; supervised education of Henry VI

St Mary's, Warwick, T

BEAUFORT, Edmund: ?-1455 K
2nd Duke of Somerset. Killed in 1st Battle of St Albans

St Alban's Cathedral, Lady Chapel, site unknown

BEAUMONT, Cardinal Henry: 1377-1447
Judge of Joan of Arc

Winchester Cathedral T

BEAUMONT, Francis: c1584-1616
Dramatist

WA Poets' Corner

BEAUMONT, Sir John: 1582-1627
Poet, brother of the above

WA Poets' Corner

BECKET, Gilbert: ? - ?
Father of Thomas

Chapel, St Paul's Cathedral, London, YD D

BECKET, Saint Thomas: 1118-1170 M
AC 1162-1170 martyred

Canterbury Cathedral TD 1538

BEDE, The Venerable: c673-735
Saint, historian

Durham Cathedral, buried 1020,
T 1831

BEERBOHM, Sir Max: 1872-1956
Caricaturist and writer

St Paul's Cathedral, London

BEETHOVEN, Ludwig van: 1770-1827
Composer

Originally Währing Cemetery,
moved to Central Cemetery,
Vienna 1888

BEETON, Mrs Isabella: 1836-1865
'Isobel', cookery books

West Norwood Cemetery, London

BEHN, Aphra: 1640-1689
Playwright, spy

WA East Cloister

BELL, Alexander Graham: 1847-1922
Telephone

Baddeck, Nova Scotia

BELL, Sir Charles: 1774-1842
Solved mystery of the human nervous system

Old churchyard, Hallow, Worcs.
MON in new church of St Philip
and St James.

BELLOC, Hilaire (Joseph Hilary Pierre): 1870-1953
French born writer

RC Cemetery, West Grimstead,
West Sussex

BENNETT, (Enoch) Arnold: 1867-1931
Novelist

Burslem Cemetery, Stoke-On-Trent,
Staffs

BERKELEY, George: 1685-1753
Irish bishop and philosopher

Christ Church, Oxford

BERNARD, Saint of Clairvaux: 1090-1153

Near Clairvaux, France

BESANT, Sir Walter: 1836-1901
Historian

St John's, Hampstead, London YD

BESS of HARDWICK: 1518-1608
Elizabeth of Talbot, Countess of Shrewsbury

Derby Cathedral T

BESSEMER, Sir Henry: 1813-1898
Steel processing

Norwood Cemetery, London

BETJEMAN, Sir John: 1906-1984
Poet

St Enodoc's, Trebetherick,
Cornwall, MEM WA, Poet's Corner

BETTERTON, Thomas: c1635-1710
Actor

WA East Cloister

BEVIN, Ernest: 1881-1951
Statesman

WA Nave

BLACK DEATH: 1348-1357
50,000 victims

Near Charterhouse Cemetery,
London

BLACKMORE, R D: 1825-1900
(Richard Doddridge), novelist

Teddington Cemetery, Richmond,
London

BLACKSTONE, Sir William: 1723-1780
Jurist

St Peter's, Wallingford, Berks

BLAIR, Eric: 1903-1950
'George Orwell', novelist and essayist

All Saints, Sutton Courtenay, Oxon

BLAKE, Admiral Robert: 1599-1657
Known as 'Father of the Royal Navy'

Originally in Henry VII Chapel,
reburied in St Margaret's YD,
MEM WA, South Choir Aisle

BLAKE, William: 1757-1827
Poet, artist

Bunhill Fields, London. MEM WA
Poets' Corner

BLIGH, Admiral William: 1754-1817
Captain of the 'Bounty'

St Mary's, Lambeth T

BLONDIN, Charles: 1824-1897
(Jean François Gravelet) Crossed
Niagra Falls on a tightrope

Kensal Green Cemetery, London

BLOOD, Colonel Thomas: 1618-1680
Stole Crown Jewels

Christ Church, Broadway,
Westminster, London D

BLORE, Edward: 1787-1879
Architect

Highgate Cemetery, London T

BODLEY, Sir Thomas: 1545-1613
Founder of the Bodleian Library

Merton College Chapel, Oxford,
MEM

BOLEYN, George: ?-1536 X
Viscount Rochford. Brother of Anne Boleyn

St Peter-ad-Vincula,
Tower of London

BOLEYN, Sir Thomas: 1477-1539
Earl of Wiltshire, father of Anne

St Peter, Hever, Kent T B

BOLTON, Prior: 1470-1532
Master of Works, Henry VII Chapel

St Bartholomew's, London

BOOTH, Barton: 1681-1733
Actor

St Laurence Cowley, near
Uxbridge, Middlesex, MEM WA
Poets' Corner

BOOTH, William: 1829-1912
Founder of the Salvation Army

Abney Park Cemetery, Stoke
Newington, London.
Bust WA, St George's Chapel

BOSHAM, Herbert de: ?-1186
Becket's secretary

Holy Trinity, Bosham, West Sussex.

BOSWELL, James: 1740-1795
Biographer of Dr Johnson

Family mausoleum, Old Kirk,
Auchinleck, Ayrshire

BOTHWELL, James Hepburn
Earl of (see **Royal Section**)

BOULT, Sir Adrian: 1889-1983
Conductor

Body to medical science.
MEM WA North Choir Aisle

BOURBON, Duke of: ?-1443
Prisoner of Agincourt

Greyfriars, London D

BOWLDLER, Thomas: 1754-1825
'Bowdlerize'

All Saints, Oystermouth, West
Glamorgan YD

BOYCE, William: c1710-1779
Composer

St Paul's Cathedral, London

BOYLE, Robert: 1627-1691
Philosopher and chemist

St Martin in the Fields, London
YD D

BRACTON, Henry de: c1210 -1268
(or Bratten or Bretton) First to treat the whole
of English Law in a systematic way

Exeter Cathedral, plaque

BRANDON, Charles: 1484-1545
Duke of Suffolk, 2nd husband of Henry VIII's
sister, Mary

St George's, Windsor G

BRANDON, Richard: ?-1649
Executioner of Charles I, Earl of Holland
& Duke of Hamilton, all with the same axe.

St Mary Matfelon, Whitechapel,
London YD

BRASSEY, Thomas: 1805-1870
Railway builder in England, France, the Crimea,
India, the Alps, Argentina, Canada and Australia

St Laurence, Catsfield,
East Sussex, YD

BRAY, Sir Reginald: ?-1503
Benefactor Henry VII Chapel

St George's, Windsor

BRIDGES, Robert: 1844-1930
Poet laureate, 1913-1930

St Peter and St Paul, Yattendon,
Berks YD

BRITTEN, Benjamin: 1913-1976
Baron Britten of Aledburgh, composer

St Peter and St Paul, Aldeburgh, Suffolk YD. MEM WA North Choir Aisle

BRONTË, Anne: 1820-1849
Novelist

St Mary, Scarborough, North Yorkshire YD. MEM WA Poets' Corner

BRONTË, Charlotte: 1816-1855
Novelist

St Michael and All Angels, Haworth, West Yorkshire. MEM WA Poets' Corner

BRONTË, Emily: 1818-1848
Novelist

St Michael and All Angels, Haworth, West Yorkshire. MEM WA Poets' Corner

BROUGHAM, Henry Peter: 1788-1868
1st Baron Brougham and Vaux, Lord Chancellor, horse-drawn 'brougham' named after him

Cannes, France G

BROWN, Lancelot: 1715-1783
Known as 'Capability Brown', lanscape gardener

St Peter and St Paul, Fenstanton, Cambridgeshire YD

BROWNE, Sir Anthony: 1526-1592
Lord Montague. Court official under Edward VI, Mary and Elizabeth

Midhurst Parish Church, Sussex T. MEM removed to Easebourne, West Sussex 1851

BROWNE, Sir Anthony: 1500-1548
Father of above. Henry VIII's Master of the Horse, given Battle Abbey by Henry

St Mary the Virgin, Battle, East Sussex, T by Torrigiani

BROWNING, Elizabeth Barrett: 1806-1861
Poet

Protestant Cemetery, Florence, Italy

BROWNING, Robert: 1812-1889
Poet

WA Poets' Corner

BRUNEL, Isambard Kingdom: 1806-1859
Iron ships, bridges, railways, Thames tunnel

Kensal Green Cemetery, London. MEM WA Nave window

BUCHER, Martin: 1491-1551
Religious reformer

Gt St Mary's Cambridge. Disinterred 1557, brass plate tells story

BUCHAN, John: 1875-1940
Author, 1st Baron Tweedsmuir. Governor-General of Canada

St Thomas of Canterbury, Elsfield, Oxon YD

BUNHILL FIELDS, London

Resting place for cartloads of bones removed from St Paul's Charnel House in 1547; burial place for Nonconformists

BUNYAN, John: 1628-1688
Author, 'Pilgrim's Progress'

Bunhill Fields, London T, 1862.
MEM WA North Transept window

BURBAGE, Richard: c1567-1619
Actor, the first Hamlet

St Leonard's, Shoreditch, London

BURDETT-COUTTS, Angela: 1814-1906
Baroness Burdett-Coutts: philanthropist

WA Nave

BURGHLEY, Lord
See **Cecil**, William

BURGOYNE, General John: 1722-1792
C-in-C British Forces in American Revolution

WA North Cloister

BURKE, Edmund: 1729-1797
Parliamentarian

St Mary and All Saints,
Beaconsfield, Bucks

BURKE, Walter: 1729-1815
Nelson died in his arms

All Saints, Wouldham, Kent, YD

BURNEY, Dr Charles: 1726-1814
Music historian

Chelsea Hospital, London, old
cemetery. MEM WA North Choir
Aisle.

BURNS, Robert: 1759-1796
Poet

St Michael's, Dumfries, YD.
MEM WA Poets' Corner

BURTON, Sir Richard: 1821-1890
Explorer

St Mary Magdalen's, Mortlake,
London YD T

BURTON, Richard: 1925-1984
Actor

Celigny, Switzerland

BUTLER, Lady Eleanor: ?-1466
Edward IV's betrothal to her caused his
children to be declared bastards

Church of White Friars, Norwich,
Norfolk D

BUTLER, Samuel: 1612-1680
Author 'Hudibras'

St Paul's, Covent Garden, London

BUTLER, Samuel: 1835-1902
Author 'Erewhon'

Cremated at Woking and ashes
dispersed

BUXHILL (or Boxhill), Sir Alan: 1323-1381
Constable of the Tower of London. Participated
in murder of Haule(y) qv

Old St Paul's Cathedral, London D

BYNG, Admiral John: 1704-1757 X
Shot as example to the others after losing
the Battle of Minorca

All Saints, Southill, Beds

BYRD, William: 1543-1623
Composer

St Peter and St Paul,
Stondon Massey, Essex, (possibly)

BYRON, George Gordon: 1788-1824
6th Baron Byron, poet

St Mary Magdalen, Hucknall
Torkard, Notts, vault. Coffin
opened 1938, face recognizable,
MEM WA Poets' Corner

CAESAR, Sir Julius: 1558-1636
Chancellor of the Exchequer for James I

St Helen's, Bishopsgate, London T

CALVERT, George: 1580-1632
1st Baron Baltimore, founded Maryland,
named for Charles I's Queen

St Dunstan in the West, Fleet
Street, London D

CALVIN, John: 1509-1564
French theologian and reformer

Geneva, Switzerland,
site unknown

CAMDEN, William: 1551-1623
Historian

WA Poets' Corner

CAMOYS, Thomas de, 5th Baron: ?-1420
Commanded left wing of English Army
at Agincourt

St George, Trotton, West Sussex T

CAMPION, Thomas: 1567-1620
Poet

St Dunstan in the West, Fleet
Street, London D

CANNING, Charles: 1812-1862
1st Earl Canning, third son of
George Canning

WA North Transept MEM

CANNING, George: 1770-1827
PM 1827, father of Charles Canning

WA North Transept MEM

CANNING, Stratford: 1786-1880
1st Viscount Stratford de Radcliffe,
cousin of George Canning

St Alban, Frant, East Sussex YD.
MEM WA North Transept.

CANTELUPE, St Thomas de: 1218-1282
Bishop of Hereford

Hereford Cathedral T

CANTELUPE, Walter: ?-1266
Bishop of Worcester

Worcester Cathedral

CARDIGAN, 7th Earl of: 1797-1868
(James Thomas Brudenell).
Charge of the Light Brigade

St Peter, Deene, Northants T

CAREW, Sir Nicholas: 1505-1539X
Friend of Henry VIII and Master of Horse.
Beheaded for treason

St Botolph, Aldgate, London D

CAREY, William: 1761-1834
Baptist missionary

Serampur, India.
MEM lectern in WA

CARLILE, Wilson: 1847-1942
Founder of the Church Army

St Paul's Cathedral, London

CARLYLE, Thomas: 1795-1881
Historian.

Ecclefechan, Dumfriers and
Galloway

CARLYLE'S DOG, NERO: ?-1841

24, Cheyne Row, London

CARNEGIE, Andrew: 1835-1918
Philanthropist – libraries

North Tarrytown, New York, USA

CARROLL, Lewis: 1832-1898
(Charles Dodgson) Author of
'Alice in Wonderland'

The Mount Cemetery, Guildford,
Surrey MEM WA Poets' Corner

CARTE, Richard D'Oyly: 1844-1901
Promoter English Opera

St Andrew, Fairlight, Hastings,
East Sussex YD

CARTERET, Sir George: ?-1680
Governor of Jersey, New Jersey, USA,
Carteret Borough named after him

St Mary, Haynes, Beds T

CASAUBON, Isaac: 1559-1614
Classical scholar

WA Poets' Corner

CASAUBON, Meric: 1599-1671
Scholar

Canterbury Cathedral

CATESBY, William: c1440-1485
'The cat, the rat and Lovell the dog'

St Leodegarius, Ashby St Ledgers,
Northants B

CAVELL, Edith: 1865-1915 X
Nurse, executed by Germans
in World War I

Originally Brussels, moved 1919 to
Norwich Cathedral, YD

CAVENDISH, George: c1500-c1561
Cardinal Wolsey's secretary

St Mary the Virgin, Glemsford,
Suffolk YD (possibly)

CAVENDISH, Sir William: c1505-1557
Husband of Bess of Hardwick

Old St Paul's, London D

CAVENDISH, Henry: 1731-1810
Physicist

Derby Cathedral

CAXTON, William: 1422-1491
First English printer

St Margaret's Westminster,
London YD, MEM WA exit of
Poets' Corner

CECIL, Robert: 1563-1612
1st Earl of Salisbury, son of Burghley

St Etheldreda, Hatfield, Herts YD

CECIL, Robert: 1830-1903
3rd Marquis of Salisbury, PM three times
1885, 1886-1892 & 1895-1902

St Etheldreda, Hatfields, Herts YD.
Cenotaph in WA Nave

CECIL, William: 1520-1598
Baron Burghley

St Michael's, Stamford, Lincs T

CHALLONER, Richard: 1691-1781
RC Bishop revised Douai Bible

Originally Anglican church at
Milton Nr Abingdon, Oxon,
moved to Westminster Cathedral
1946

CHAMBERLAIN, Neville: 1869-1940
PM 1937-1940

WA Nave

CHAMBERS, Sir William: 1723-1796
Architect

WA Poets' Corner

CHAMBERS, William: 1800-1883
Encyclopaedia

St Andrew's, Peebles, Scotland,
YD

CHANTREY, Sir Francis: 1781-1841
Sculptor, 'Chantrey bequest for purchase of art'

St James, Norton, Sheffield,
Yorks G

CHAPLIN, Sir Charles: 1889-1977
Comedian

Cursier-sur-Vevey, Switzerland

CHAPMAN, George: 1559-1634
Translator of Homer

St Giles in the Fields, London

CHAUCER, Alice: 1404-1474
Granddaughter of poet,
wife of 1st Duke of Suffolk

St Mary the Virgin, Ewelme,
Oxon T

CHAUCER, Geoffrey: c1343-1400
Poet

WA Poets' Corner

CHAUCER, Thomas: 1367-1434
Son of poet, father of Alice

St Mary the Virgin, Ewelme,
Oxon T

CHESTERTON, GK : 1874-1936
(Gilbert Keith) Author

Beaconsfield RC Cemetery, Bucks

CHIPPENDALE, Thomas: 1718-1779
Furniture maker

St Martin-in-the-Fields, London D

CHRISTIE, Dame Agatha: 1890-1976
Novelist

St Mary's, Cholsey, Berks

CHRISTIE, James: 1730-1803
Founder of auctioneers

St James's, Piccadilly, London

CHURCH CAT, Tom: 1912-1927
15 years church cat, St Mary Redcliffe

St Mary Redcliffe, Bristol G

CHURCHILL, John: 1650-1722
1st Duke of Marlborough,
soldier & statesman

Originally WA; removed 1744 to
Blenheim Palace Chapel, Oxon T

CHURCHILL, John: ?-1703
Only son of 1st Duke

King's College Chapel,
Cambridge T

CHURCHILL, Sir Winston: 1874-1965
PM during World War II 1940-1945
& 1951-1955

St Martin's, Bladon, Oxon, YD G.
MEM WA Nave and under dome
at St Paul's Cathedral, together
with memorial gates in crypt

CHURCHYARD GRIM: DOG

Buried on north side of every
ancient churchyard, to protect
the dead from the devil

CLARENDON, Earl of
See **Hyde**

CLARKSON, Thomas: 1760-1846
Abolitionist of slave trade

Playford, Suffolk

CLEMENTI, Muzio: 1752-1832
'Father of the pianoforte'

WA South Cloister

CLIVE, Robert, Baron: 1725-1774
'Clive of India'

St Marageret's Moreton Say,
Shrewsbury. MEM WA South
Choir Aisle

COBBETT, William: 1763-1835
Author 'Rural Rides'. Returned Tom Paine's
bones to England from USA

St Andrew, Farnham, Surrey YD

COBDEN, Richard: 1804-1865
Protagonist for free trade & founded of
Anti-Corn Law League. MP

St Mary Magdalene, West
Lavington, West Sussex, YD

COKE, Sir Edward: 1552-1634
Lord Coke (or Cooke), Chief Justice of England.
Walter Raleigh's prosecutor

St Mary's, Tittleshall, Norfolk

COLERIDGE, Samuel Taylor: 1772-1834
Poet, 'Ancient Mariner'

St Michael's, Highgate, London
MEM WA Poets' Corner

COLERIDGE-TAYLOR, Samuel: 1875-1912
Composer, 'Hiawatha's Wedding Feast'

Baudon Hill Cemetery, Croydon,
Surrey T

COLET, Sir Henry: ?-1510
Philanthropist. Father of 22 children
but only one survived him, see **Colet John**

St Dunstan's, Stepney, London

COLET, John: 1467-1519
Dean of St Paul's, son of Sir Henry Colet

Old St Paul's Cathedral, London D

COLLINGWOOD, Cuthbert, Lord: 1750-1810
Naval Commander

St Paul's Cathedral, London T

COLUMBUS, Christopher: 1451-1506
Naval commander, navigator

Uncertain – Ciudad Trujillo,
Dominican Republic or Seville,
Spain

COMPTON-BURNETT, Dame Ivy: 1884-1969
Novelist

Putney Vale Cemetery, London

CONGREVE, William: 1670-1729
Dramatist & poet

WA Nave MEM

CONRAD, Joseph: 1857-1924
Novelist

St Thomas RC Cemetery,
Canterbury

CONSTABLE, John: 1776-1837
Artist

St John's, Hampstead, London
YD T

COOK, Captain James: 1728-1779 K
Navigator.

Kona, Hawaii, where he was
killed. MEM WA South Cloister.
Monuments at Tahiti & Kona,
Hawaii and Whitby & Marton,
Yorks

COOKE, Edward: ?-1652

St Bartholomew the Great,
London. Tomb 'wept' as its
marble oozed water – cured by
central heating

COOPER, Anthony Ashley: 1621-1683
1st Earl of Shaftesbury.
Habeas Corpus Act of 1679

St Giles, Wimborne, St Giles,
Dorset

COOPER, Anthony Ashley: 1801-1885
7th Earl of Shaftesbury, reformer

St Giles, Wimborne St Giles,
Dorset. Statue WA Nave

COOPER, Dame Gladys: 1888-1971
Actress

Hampstead Cemetery, London

COPLEY, John Singleton the Elder: 1738-1815
Artist

Highgate Cemetery, London

CORELLI, Marie: 1855-1924
Nom de plume, born Mary Mackay. Novelist

Stratford-upon-Avon Cemetery,
Warwickshire

CORNWALLIS, Charles: 1738-1805
1st Marquess and 2nd Earl: surrendered at
Yorktown, Virginia. Governor-General, India

Ghazipore, India, MEM St Paul's
Cathedral, London

COTMAN, John Sell: 1782-1842
Artist & draughtsman

St John's Wood, London YD

COTTON, Sir Robert Bruce: 1571-1631
Cottonian Manuscripts

St Mary, Conington, Cambs

COVERDALE, Miles: 1488-1568
Bible translator

Originally St Bartholomew-by-the-
Exchange. Reburied 1840
St Magnus the Martyr,
London MEM

COWARD, Sir Noël: 1899-1973
Writer and entertainer

Jamaica, West Indies.
MEM WA South Choir Aisle

COWLEY, Abraham: 1618-1667
Poet

WA Poets' Corner MON

COWPER, William: 1731-1800
Poet

St Nicholas, East Dereham,
Norfolk. MEM WA St George's
Chapel window

CRANMER, Archbishop Thomas: 1489-1556 X
AC 1533-1556

Burnt at the stake, Oxford

CRAPPER, Thomas: 1837-1910
Plumber, developed modern WC cistern

Crystal Palace District Cemetery,
Nr Beckenham, London. 3
manhole covers with name on
them in WA cloisters

CRIPPS, Sir (Richard) Stafford: 1889-1952
Politician

Sapperton, Cemetery, Glos. MEM
St Paul's Cathedral, London

CROMWELL, Anne: 1661-1727
Daughter of Oliver Cromwell's 3rd son

St George's Cemetery,
Bloomsbury, London

CROMWELL, Bridget: 1624-1681
Eldest daughter of Oliver Cromwell

St Anne's, Blackfriars, London

CROMWELL, Mary: 1636-1712
6th child of Oliver Cromwell

St George's Cemetery,
Bloomsbury, London

CROMWELL, Oliver: 1599-1658
Lord Protector of England

Originally WA Henry VII Chapel.
Removed 1661 &beheaded; body
buried at Tyburn, London, head
buried in Sydney Sussex College,
Cambridge, 1960

CROMWELL, Ralph: 1394-1455
Lord High Treasurer of England

Holy Trinity, Tattershall, Lincs

CROMWELL, Richard: 1626-1712
3rd son of Oliver Cromwell. Succeeded
his father as Lord Protector of England

All Saints, Hursley, Hants

CROMWELL, Thomas: 1484-1540 X
Earl of Essex. Wolsey's secretary
and Henry VIII's Chancellor

St Peter-ad-Vincula, Tower of
London

CROSBY, Sir John: ?-1475
Built Crosby Hall

St Helen's, Bishopsgate, London T

CRUDEN, Alexander: 1701-1770
Cruden's Bible Concordance

Southwark Cathedral YD

CRUFT, Charles: 1852-1939
Founder of dog show

Highgate Cemetery, London

CUBITT, Thomas: 1788-1855
Built much of London; upper Woburn Place,
Tavistock Street, East wing of Buckingham
Palace, Belgravia, etc

Denbies, near Dorking, Surrey

CUTHBERT, Saint: c634-687
Anglo-Saxon Churchman and missionary

Originally Lindisfarne, then to
Durham Cathedral in 999 G

D'ABERNON, Sir John: ?-1277

St Mary's, Stoke D'Abernon,
Surrey. Oldest brass in England
which is 6 feet, 6 inches long

DANCE George, the Elder: 1700-1768
Architect

St Luke's, Old Street, London D

DANCE George, the Younger: 1741-1825
Architect

St Paul's Cathedral, London

D'ARCY, Thomas: 1467-1537 X
Baron of Templehurst. Official under
Henry VII and Henry VIII

St Botolph's, Aldersgate,
London D

DARLING, Grace: 1815-1842
With father rescued shipwrecked persons

St Aidan's, Bamburgh,
Northumberland MON YD

DART, John: ?-1730
Author of 'Westmonasterium' or
'The History and Antiquities of The Abbey
Church of St Peter's Westminster

St Peter's, Yateley, Hants

DARTMOUTH, 2nd Earl: see **Legge**

DARWIN, Charles: 1809-1882
'Origin of the Species'

WA Nave

DASHWOOD, Sir Frances: 1708-1781
15th Baron le Dispencer Hell-Fire Club

West Wycombe, Bucks,
Mausoleum

D'AVENANT, Sir William: 1606-1668
Dramatist and poet

WA Poets' Corner

**DAVIS, Christine,
changed to DAVIES, Christian:** 1667-1739
Woman soldier who served as a man, wounded
at Ramillies in War of Spanish Succession

Royal Chelsea Hospital burying
ground

DAVISON, Emily Wilding: 1872-1913 K
Suffragette killed by throwing herself
in front of the King's horse at the Derby

Morpeth Cemetery,
Northumberland

DAVY, Sir Humphy: 1778-1829
Chemist

Plain-Palais Cemetery, Geneva,
Switzerland T MEM WA St
Andrew's Chapel

DAY-LEWIS, Cecil: 1904-1972
poet and novelist

St Michael's, Stinsford, Dorset YD

DE BURGH, Hubert: ?-1243
Earl of Kent

Blackfriars Church, London D

DE CLARE, Elizabeth: 1292-1360
Founder Clare College, Cambridge

Minories Church, London D

DE CLARE, Gilbert: 1180 -1230

Tewkesbury Abbey

DEE, Dr John: 1527-1608
Elizabeth's astrologer

St Mary's, Mortlake, London

DEFOE, Daniel: 1660-1731
Author

Bunhill Fields, London

DE GAULLE, General Charles: 1890-1970
French general and 1st President of 5th Republic

Colombey-les-deux-Eglises, France

DE LA MARE, Walter: 1872-1956
Poet

St Paul's Cathedral, London

DELIUS, Frederick: 1862-1934
Composer

Originally in graveyard at Grez-
sur-Loing, France. Moved one year
later to St Peter's, Limpsfield,
Surrey YD

DE QUINCEY, Thomas: 1785-1859
Author 'Confessions of an English Opium Eater'

St Cuthbert's Edinburgh YD

DE SADE, Marquis: 1740-1814
(Donatien, Alphonse, François)
sadism derived from his name

Charenton, France, , remains later
exhumed and scattered

DE VALENCE: see **Pembroke**

DE VERE, Aubrey: 1814-1902
Poet

St Mary's, Askeaton, Co Limerick,
Ireland YD

DEVEREUX, Robert: 1566-1601 X
2nd Earl of Essex, soldier and courtier

St Peter-ad-Vincula, Tower of
London

DE WORDE, Wynkyn: ?-1535
Successor to Caxton

St Bride's, London YD

DICKENS, Charles: 1812-1879
Author

WA Poets' Corner

DICKENS FAMILY
Wife (Catherine Hogarth), parents and
Dora, his 9th child

Highgate Cemetery, London

DICKINSON, William: 1661-1725
Manager of Wren's Abbey work

WA North Transept

DIMBLEBY, Richard: 1913-1965
Broadcaster

St Peter, Lynchmere, West Sussex
YD. MEM WA South Choir Aisle

DISRAELI, Benjamin: 1804-1881
Earl of Beaconsfield: PM 1868 and1874-80
statesman and novelist

St Michael's and All Angels,
Hughenden, Bucks YD. MEM WA
North Transept

DODGSON, Charles See **Carroll, Lewis**

DONNE, John: 1572-1631
Poet, Dean of St Paul's

Old St Paul's Cathedral, London.
original effigy in present St Paul's

DORISLAUS, Isaac: 1595-1649 M
Drew up charges against Charles I

Originally WA, removed to
St Margaret's Churchyard 1661

DOUGLAS, Gavin: 1474-1522
Poet, Bishop of Dunkeld

Hospital Church of the Savoy,
London D

DOUGLAS, Sir John Sholto: 1844-1900
Marquess of Queensberry, Queensberry rules

Kinmount, Dumfries and Galloway

DOWDING, Hugh: 1882-1970
Air Chief Marshall, 1st Baron.
Commanded 'The Few' at the Battle of Britain

WA Henry VII Chapel

DOWSING, William: 1596-1679
Puritan, 'The Great Destroyer'.
Broke 200 'superstitious pictures'
(stained glass windows) in one day

All Saints', Laxfield, Suffolk

DOWSON, Ernest: 1867-1900
Poet, 'Faithful to thee, Cynara' and
'The Days of the Wine and Roses'

RC Cemetery, Lewisham London

DOYLE, Sir Arthur Conan: 1859-1930
Author, 'Sherlock Holmes'

Originally buried in grounds of his
house, Windlesham Manor,
Crowborough. 1955, removed to
All Saints' Minstead, Hants YD

DRAKE, Sir Francis: 1540-1596
Navigator and privateer

At sea off Portobelo, Panama.
MEM WA South Cloister

DRAYTON, Michael: 1563-1631
Poet

WA Poets' Corner

DRYDEN, John: 1631-1700
Poet

WA Poets' Corner

DUDLEY, Lord Guildford: ?-1554 X
Husband of Lady Jane Grey

St Peter-ad-Vincula,
Tower of London

DUDLEY, John: 1502-1553 X
Duke of Northumberland

St Peter-ad-Vincula,
Tower of London

DUDLEY, Robert: 1533-1588
Earl of Leicester

St Mary's, Warwick

DU MAURIER, Dame Daphne: 1907-1989
Novelist

Ashes scattered in grounds of
Kilmarth House, Menabilly,
Cornwall

DU MAURIER, George: 1834-1896
Author

St John's, Hampstead, London
YD T

DUNSTABLE, John: c1390-1453
Composer

St Stephen Walbrook, London D

DUNSTAN, Saint: c909-988
AC 959-988

Canterbury Cathedral

DUPPA, Brian: 1588-1662
Tutor to Charles II

WA North Ambulatory

EDEN, Sir Anthony: 1897-1977
1st Earl of Avon, PM 1955-1957

St Mary's Alvediston, Wilts YD

EINSTEIN, Albert: 1879-1955
Theoretical physicist

Cremated New Jersey (brain
removed) and ashes scattered
secretly

ELGAR, Sir Edward: 1857-1934
Composer

St Wulfstan RC Churchyard, Little Malvern, Worcs G. MEM WA North Choir Aisle

ELGIN, Thomas Bruce, 7th Earl: 1766-1841
Brought Marbles to Britain

St Mary, Maulden, Beds

ELIOT, George: 1819-1880
(Mary Ann Evans) Novelist

Highgate Cemetery, London
MEM WA Poets' Corner

ELIOT, T S (Thomas Stearns): 1888-1965
Poet

St Michael's, East Coker, Somerset, MEM WA Poets' Corner

ELLIS, Havelock: 1859-1939
Writer on sex & psychology

St Nicholas, Hindlesham, Suffolk

ENGLEHEART, George: 1750-1829
Painter of portraits & miniatures

St Anne, Kew Green, London YD

ERASMUS, Desiderius: 1466-1536
Humanist

Basel, Switzerland

EVELYN, John: 1620-1706
Diarist

St John's, Wotton, Surrey T

FABERGÉ, Peter Carl: 1846-1920
Jeweller to the Russian Court

Cannes, France

FAIRFAX, Thomas 3rd Baron: 1612-1671
Parliamentarian, won at Naseby

St James, Bilbrough, North Yorkshire

FARADAY, Michael: 1791-1867
Chemist & physicist

Highgate Cemetery, London, MEM WA Nave

FASTOLF, Sir John: 1378-1459
Possibly the original of Shakespeare's Falstaff

St Benet's, Caister-on-Sea, Norfolk

FAYED, Dodi: 1955-1997
Companion of Diana Princess of Wales

Originally Brookwood Cemetery, Surrey, moved to family home, Oxted, Surrey.

FECKENHAM, Abbot John: c1518-1585
Abbot of WA under Mary Tudor

St Peter's, Wisbech, Cambs G

FENN, Sir John: 1739-1794
Edited Paston letters

St Bartholomew, Finningham, Suffolk

FISHER, Saint John: 1469-1535 X
Bishop of Rochester

All Hallows Barking-by-the-Tower. Moved to St Peter-ad-Vincula, Tower of London

FISKE, William Meade Lindsley: 1911-1940 K
'Billy', US pilot who fought in Battle of Britain

Boxgrove Priory, West Sussex.
MEM St Paul's Cathedral Crypt

FITZALAN, Richard: 1346-1397 X
4th Earl of Arundel & Surrey

Austin Friars, London D

FITZGERALD, Edward: 1809-1883
Translated 'Rubaiyat of Omar Khayyám'

St Michael's Boulge, Suffolk YD

FITZROY, Henry: 1663-1690
1st Duke of Grafton. Illegitimate son of Charles II
by Barbara Villiers

St Genevieve, Euston, Suffolk

FLAMSTEED, John: 1646-1719
1st Astronomer Royal, founded
Greenwich Observatory

St Bartholomew's, Burstow, Surrey

FLAXMAN, John: 1755-1826
Sculptor and Draughtsman

St Pancras Old Church, London

FLEETWOOD, Charles: c1618-1692
Husband of Bridget Cromwell

Bunhill Fields, London

FLEMING, Sir Alexander: 1881-1955
Discovered penicillin

St Paul's Cathedral, London

FLETCHER, Sir Bannister: 1833-1899
Architect, author

West Hampstead Cemetery,
London

FLETCHER, John: 1579-1625
Dramatist

Southwark Cathedral, London

FLOREY, Howard Walter: 1898-1968
Baron, developer of penicillin

Marston, Oxon, MEM WA Nave

FONTEYN, Dame Margot: 1919-1991
Ballerina

Panama City
MEM WA Poets' Corner

FORMBY, George: 1904-1961
Comedian and banjoist

RC Cemetery, Warrington,
Cheshire

FOX, Charles James: 1749-1806
Statesman

WA North Transept, MEM WA
Nave

FOX, George: 1624-1691
Founder of the Quakers

Roscoe Street Old Friends burial
grounds, London

FOX, Henry: 1705-1774
1st Lord Holland father of Charles James

All Saints, Farley, Wilts

FOXE, John: 1516-1587
Author, 'Book of Martyrs'

St Giles Cripplegate, London

FOYLE, William: 1885-1963
Founder of bookshop on Charing Cross Road

Highgate Cemetery, London

FRASER, Simon: 1667-1747 X
12th Baron Lovat, Jacobite

St Peter-ad-Vincula, Tower of London

FRENCH, Sir John: 1852-1925
Earl of Ypres, C-in-C 1914-1915

St Mary the Virgin, Ripple, Kent YD

FRITH, Mary: 1584-1659
Known as 'Moll Cutpurse'

St Bride's, London

FROBISHER, Sir Martin: 1535-1594
Privateer

St Giles Cripplegate, London, viscera in St Andrew's, Plymouth

FROUDE, James Anthony: 1818-1894
Historian, 'History of England' in 12 volumes

Salcombe, Devon YD

FRY, Elizabeth: 1780-1845
Prison reformer & Quaker

Friends Cemetery, Barking (now a public garden)

FULLER, John: 1756-1834
Wealthy eccentric, built the Brightling Needles, one being an obelisk 646 feet high.

St Thomas Becket's, Brightling, East Sussex YD. An 80 foot pyramid sits over his grave where he is said to be buried sitting up holding a bottle of wine & wearing his top hat

FULLER, Thomas: 1608-1661
Preacher & author, 'Worthies of England'

St Dunstan, Cranford, Hounslow, London

FUSELI, Henry: 1741-1825
Artist

St Paul's Cathedral, London

GADDESDEN, Dr John: 1280-1361
Early GP & author 'Rosa Medicinae'

Old St Paul's Cathedral, London D

GAINSBOROUGH, Thomas: 1727-1788
Artist

St Anne's, Kew Green, London

GAITSKELL, Hugh: 1906-1963
Chancellor of the Exchequer, leader of Labour Party

St John's, Hampstead, London YD

GALILEO: 1564-1642
Astronomer, said sun did not move

Santa Croce, Florence, Italy

GALSWORTHY, John: 1867-1933
Novelist

Ashes scattered on Sussex Downs, MEM Highgate Cemetery

GAMA, Vasco da: 1469-1524
Explorer

Originally Cochin, India, moved to Lisbon, Portugal

GARDINER, Bishop Stephen: 1483-1555
Wolsey's secretary

Winchester Cathedral

GARRICK, David: 1716-1779
Actor

WA Poets' Corner MON

GASKELL, Elizabeth Cleghorn: 1810-1865
Novelist & Biographer

Unitarian Church, Knutsford,
Cheshire YD
MEM WA Poets' Corner Window

GAVESTON, Piers: ?-1312 X
Favourite of Edward II

Dominican Friary, King's Langley,
Herts D

GAY, John: 1685-1732
Poet

WA Poets' Corner
MEM now in Triforium

GETHIN, Dame Grace: c1677-1697
Author of reflections

Hollingbourne, Kent,
MEM WA South Choir Aisle

GIBBON, Edward: 1737-1794
Author, 'Decline & Fall of the Roman Empire'

St Mary & St Andrew's, Fletching,
E Sussex

GIBBONS, Christopher: 1615-1676
Son of Orlando, WA organist

WA North Cloister

GIBBONS, Grinling: 1648-1721
Wood-carver

St Paul's, Covent Garden, London

GIBBONS, Orlando: 1583-1625
Composer & WA organist

Canterbury Cathedral
MEM WA North Choir Aisle

GILBERT, Sir William Schwenck: 1836-1911
Librettist and wit (of Gilbert and Sullivan)

St John the Evangelist's,
Great Stanmore, London

GLADSTONE, William Ewart: 1809-1898
PM 1868-1872, 1880-1885 & 1886-1894

WA North Transept, statue

GODIVA, Lady: ?-1080
Supposedly rode naked through Coventry

Benedictine Monastery,
Coventry, TD

GODOLPHIN, Charles: 1651-1720
Founder of Godolphin School

WA West Cloister

GODOLPHIN, Sidney: 1645-1712
1st Earl of Godolphin. Held office under
Charles II, James II, William III & Queen Anne

WA Nave South Aisle, bust

GODWIN, William: 1756-1836
Political writer

St Peter's, Bournemouth, Dorset
YD

GOLDSMITH, Oliver: 1728-1774
Playwright, novelist & poet

The Temple church, London YD G
MEM WA Poets' Corner

GORDON, General Charles: 1833-1885 K
Known as 'Chinese Gordon' and 'Gordon
of Khartoum'

Body never found. Cenotaph in
St Paul's Cathedral, London. MEM
WA North West Tower

GORDON, Lord George: 1751-1793
Popery riots of 1780

St James's, London D. Church site
covered by Euston Station

GOWER, John: c1325-1408
Poet

Southwalk Cathedral T

GOYA, Francisco: 1746-1828
Artist

Originally buried in Bordeaux
removed 1919 to San Antonio
Church, Madrid, Spain minus head

GRACE, Dr W G: 1848-1915
Cricketer

Crystal Palace District Cemetery,
Beckenham, London

GRANVILLE, Christine: 1915-1952
WWII resistance. GM, CBE, Croix de Guerre avec
Palmes. Real name Countess Krystyne Skerbek.
Murdered by ship's steward.

RC Cemetery, Kensal Green,
London

GRAY, Thomas: 1716-1771
Poet

St Giles', Stoke Poges, Bucks T
MEM WA Poets' Corner

GREENE, Graham: 1904-1991
Writer

Corseau-sur-vevey, Switzerland

GRENVILLE, Admiral Sir Richard: 1541-1591
'Flores in the Azores'

Died on Spanish flagship, buried
at sea

GRESHAM, Sir Thomas: 1519-1579
Banker

St Helen's, Bishopsgate, London T

GREW, Nehemiah: 1641-1712
Astronomer, botanist, discovered sex of flowers

St Mary's, Cheshunt, Herts YD

GREY, Sir Anthony: ?-1480
Elizabeth Woodville's brother-in-law

St Alban's Cathedral B

GREY, Catherine: 1538-1568
Countess of Hertford, sister of Lady Jane Grey

Salisbury Cathedral T

GREY, Henry: ?-1554 X
Marquess of Dorset, father of Jane

St Peter-ad-Vincula, Tower of
London. Head in St Botolph's,
Aldgate

GREY, Lord Thomas: ?-1554 X
Uncle of Jane

All Hallows by the Tower, London

GRIMALDI, Joseph: 1778-1837
Clown

St James's, Pentonville, London YD

GROSSESTESTE, Robert: c1175-1253
Scientist, philosopher, bishop

Lincoln Cathedral G

GUNDULF, Bishop of Rochester: 1024-1108

Rochester Cathedral

GUY, Thomas: 1644-1724
Founder Guy's Hospital, London

Guy's Hospital Chapel

GWYNN, Nell: 1650-1687
Mistress of Charles II, mother of Duke of St Albans

St Martin in the Fields, London D

HAIG, Douglas: 1861-1928
1st Earl, Field Marshal World War I

Dryburgh Abbey, Roxbughshire,
Scotland G

HAKLUYT, Richard: c1552-1616
Father of English geographers

WA South Transept, exact site
unknown

HALES, Dr Stephen: 1677-1761
Botanist, physiologist, invented ways to
ventilate ships and prisons

St Mary, Teddington, London
MEM WA South Transept

HALLÉ, Sir Charles: 1819-1895
Conductor

RC Cemetery, Salford, Lancs

HALLEY, Edmund: 1656-1742
Astronomer

St Margaret Lee, Nr Lewisham, YD
MEM WA South Cloister

HAMPDEN, John: 1594-1643
Cromwell supporter, statesmen

St Mary Magdalene's,
Great Hampden, Bucks

HANDEL, George Frideric: 1685-1759
Composer

WA Poets' Corner MEM

HANSARD, Luke: 1752-1828
Printer to House of Commons

St Giles in the Fields, London
MEM

HANSOM, Joseph: 1803-1882
Architect, inventor of the Hansom cab

RC Church St Thomas of
Canterbury, Fulham, London

HANWAY, Jonas: 1712-1786
First Englishman to carry umbrella, philanthropist

St Mary, Hanwell, Ealing, London
YD. MEM WA North Transept

HARDY, Thomas: 1840-1928
Novelist and poet

WA Poets' Corner, heart in
Stinsford, Dorset

HARRISON, John: 1693-1776
Clock maker, determined Longitude

St John's Hampstead, Old
Churchyard. MEM WA Nave

HARTE, Francis Brett: 1836-1902
American novelist

St Peter's, Frimley, Surrey YD T

HARVARD, John: 1607-1638
His 260 books and half his estate helped
to found Harvard College, now University

Charlestown, Mass, USA

HARVEY, Dr William: 1578-1657
Discovered blood circulation

St Andrew's Hempstead, Essex

HASTINGS, Warren: 1732-1818
Governor-General, India

St Peter's, Daylesford, Glos
MEM WA North Transept

HASTINGS, Lord William: 1430-1483 X
Executed by Richard III

St George's Chapel, Windsor,
Chantry

HATTON, Sir Christopher: 1540-1591
Chancellor to Elizabeth I

Old St Paul's Cathedral, London

HATTON, Sir Christopher: 1581-1619
Cousin and successor to the above

WA North Ambulatory,
MEM now in Triforium

HAULE(Y), Robert: ?-1378 M
Murdered in WA

WA Poets' Corner

HAWKSMOOR, Nicholas: 1661-1736
Architect & pupil of Wren

St Botolph's, Shenley, Herts YD G

HAYDN, Franz Joseph: 1732-1809
Composer

Originally buried Hundsturm YD,
Vienna. Removed to Eisenstadt,
skull in museum reunited with
body in 1954

HAZLITT, William: 1788-1830
Essayist

St Anne's, Wardour Street,
London YD (now garden)

HEINE, Heinrich: 1797-1856
Poet

Montmatre, Paris

HÉLOÏSE (of Abelard & Héloïse): 1098-1164

Père Lachaise Cemetery, Paris

HEMANS, Mrs Felicia Dorothea: 1793-1835
Poet, 'Boy stood on the Burning Deck'

St Anne's Dublin

HENLEY, W.H: 1849-1903
(William Ernest) Poet 'Invictus'

St John the Baptist, Cockayne
Hatley, Beds, YD

HENTY, George Alfred: 1832-1902
Boys' stories

Brompton Cemetery, Kensington,
London

HERBERT, Edward: 1583-1648
1st Baron, philosopher, poet, diplomat

St Giles in the Fields, London

HERBERT, George: 1593-1633
Poet

St Andrew's, Bemerton, Wilts
MEM WA St George's Chapel
window

HERBERT, Mary: 1561-1621
Countess of Pembroke

Salisbury Cathedral T

HERNE, Thomas: ?-1817
Artist

St James's, Bushey, Herts YD

HERRICK, Robert: 1591-1674
Poet

St George, Dean Prior, Devon, YD
MEM WA Poets' Corner window

HERSCHEL, Caroline: 1750-1848
Discovered 8 comets, sister of William

Gartenmeinde, Hanover, Germany
YD

HERSCHEL, Sir John: 1792-1871
Astronomer

WA Nave North Aisle

HERSCHEL, Sir William: 1738-1822
Discovered Uranus, father of John

St Laurence's, Upton, Berks
MEM WA Nave

HESS, Dame Myra: 1890-1966
Pianist

Golders Green Cemetery, London

HILL, Octavia: 1838-1912
Social housing pioneer

Holy Trinity, Crockham Hill, Kent
YD MON in church

HILL, Sir Rowland: 1795-1879
Inventor penny postage

WA St Paul's Chapel MEM,
MEM Highgate

HILLIARD, Nicholas: 1547-1619
Painter of miniatures

St Martin in the Fields, London D

HOBBES, Thomas: 1588-1679
Philosopher

St John the Baptist's, Ault,
Hucknall, Derbyshire

HOGARTH, William: 1697-1764
Artist and engraver

St Lawrence's , Chiswick, London
YD T

HOLBEIN, Hans, the Younger: 1497-1543
Artist to Henry VIII

St Katherine Cree, London D

HOLLAND, Lady Elizabeth Vassal Fox: 1770-1845
Mistress of Holland House

St Andrew's, Ampthill, Beds T

HOLLAND, Henry Richard Vassal Fox: 1773-1840
3rd Baron, introduced bill to abolish hanging
for stealing

St Andrew's, Ampthill, Beds T

HOLLAND, Lady Margaret: ?-1439
Married John of Gaunt's, son John Beaufort,
Earl of Somerset; secondly Thomas Duke of Clarence,
brother of Henry V

Canterbury Cathedral.
All three buried together T

HOLLAR, Wenceslaus: 1607-1677
Engraver

St Margaret's, Westminster Abbey,
London YD MEM Southwark
Cathedral

HOLST, Gustav: 1874-1934
Composer

Chichester Cathedral

HOME OF THE HIRSEL, Baron, Alexander Frederick
Douglas-Home: 1903-1995 Life Peer 1974.
Disclaimed inherited peerages on becoming
PM from 1963 to 1964

Lennel, Coldstream, Berwicks,
Scotland YD

HOOD, Thomas: 1799-1845
Poet

Kensal Green Cemetery, London

HOOK, Walter Farquhar: 1798-1875
Dean of Chichester. Urged school for all children.
Proposed limit of 10 hour working day.

St Nicholas, Mid Lavant, West
Sussex YD

HOOKE, Robert: 1635-1703
Philosopher

St Helen's, Bishopsgate, London
MEM WA Lantern

HOOKER, Sir Joseph: 1817-1911
Botanist, director of Kew Gardens

St Anne's, Kew Green, London

HOPKINS, Gerard Manley: 1844-1889
Jesuit poet

Glasnevin Cemetery, Dublin
MEM WA Poets' Corner

HOUSMAN, A E (Alfred Edward): 1859-1936
Scholar and poet

St Laurence's, Ludlow, Salop, YD
MEM WA Poets' Corner window

HOWARD, Charles: 1536-1624
2nd Baron Howard of Effingham, Earl of
Nottingham, Lord High Admiral, commandeered
English Fleet against Spanish Armada

St Mary Magdalene's, Reigate,
Surrey

HOWARD, Henry: 1517-1547 X
Earl of Surrey. The English sonnet

Originally All Hallows Barking by
the Tower, moved 1614 to St
Michael's, Framlingham, Suffolk T

HOWARD, John: 1726-1790
First advocate of prison reform

Stepanovka, Russia.
Statue St Paul's Cathedral, London

HOWARD, Katherine: ?-1535
Duchess of Norfolk

St Mary's Lambeth, London B

HOWARD, Saint Philip: 1557-1595
1st Earl of Arundel

Originally Tower of London,
moved to Arundel 1624 T

HOWARD, Thomas: 1536-1572 X
4th Duke of Norfolk

St Peter-ad-Vincula, Tower of
London

HOWARD, William: 1510-1573
1st Baron Howard of Effingham
Lord High Admiral

St Mary Magdalene's, Reigate,
Surrey G

HOWE, Augustus: 1725-1758 K
3rd Viscount Howe. Killed at Ticonderoga,
New York State

Trout Brook, Nr Ticonderoga,
NY USA. MEM WA North West
Tower, given by Massachusetts Bay
Colony

HOWE, General William: 1729-1814
5th Viscount Howe. Commanded British
at Bunker Hill

Twickenham cemetery
(now a park), London

HOYLE, Edmond: 1672-1769
Renowned writer on games

Old Marylebone, London YD, D

HUDDLESTON, Father John: 1608-1698
Attended at death of Charles II

St Mary-le-Strand, London

HUGO, Victor: 1802-1885
Author 'Les Miserables'

Pantheon, Paris

HUME, David: 1711-1776
Philosopher, historian

Calton Hill burial ground,
Edinburgh T

HUNSDON, Henry Carey: c1525-1596
1st Baron, Cousin of Elizabeth I

WA St John the Baptist Chapel,
largest MON in WA. 36 feet high

HUNT, (James Henry) Leigh: 1784-1859
Critic, poet

Kensal Green Cemetery, London
MON

HUNT, Roger: ?-1433
Speaker when Parliament sat in
WA Chapter House

St Mary's, Roxton, Beds

HUNTER, Dr John: 1728-1793
Founder of modern surgery

Originally St Martin in the Fields,
removed 1859 to WA Nave North
Aisle B

HUNTSMAN, Benjamin: 1704-1776
Inventor of crucible (Sheffield) steel

Hill Top Chapel, Attercliffe, West
Yorkshire, YD

HUXLEY, Thomas: 1825-1895
Biologist

Finchley Cemetery, London

HYDE, Edward: 1609-1674
1st Earl of Clarendon, statesman

WA North Ambulatory

INGE, William: 1860-1954
Dean of St Paul's

St Agatha, Brightwell-cum-Sotwell, Oxon, YD T

IRVING, Sir Henry: 1838-1905
Actor, manager

WA Poets' Corner

JAMES, Henry: 1843-1916
American writer, British subject

Cambridge, Mass, USA
MEM WA Poets' Corner

JEFFREYS, George: 1648-1689
1st Baron, known as the 'hanging judge', 320 executed at Bloody Assizes

Originally Tower of London moved to St Mary, Aldermanbury, 1692. Church bombed WWII and reconstructed at Fulton, Miss USA

JEKYLL, Gertrude: 1843-1932
Gardener, silver engraver, wood-carver, embroiderer, sign-painter & quilter

St John the Baptist, Busbridge, Surrey

JELLICOE, Admiral John: 1859-1935
1st Earl Jellicoe

St Paul's Cathedral, London T

JENNER, Edward: 1749-1823
Discovered smallpox vaccine

St Mary's, Berkely, Glos YD

JEROME, Jerome Klapka: 1859-1927
Author 'Three Men in a Boat'

St Mary the Virgin, Ewelme, Oxon YD G

JOAN of ARC, Saint: c1412-1431
Burnt at Rouen, rehabilitated

Ashes thrown into Seine

JOHNSON, Elizabeth: 1688-1752
Dr Johnson's wife

Bromley, Parish Church Kent

JOHNSON, Dr Samuel: 1709-1784
Lexicographer

WA Poets' Corner, MON
MEM St Paul's Cathedral, London

JONES, Christopher: ?-1622
Captain of the 'Mayflower'

St Mary's, Rotherhithe, London, site unknown. MEM window

JONES, Inigo: 1573-1652
Architect, Banqueting hall, Whitehall

St Benet, Paul's Wharf, London D

JONSON, Ben: 1574-1637
Dramatist, buried upright

WA Nave, MEM Poets' Corner

JOSEPH, Saint: 1st century
Joseph of Arimathea

Glastonbury Abbey, supposedly

JOULE, James Prescott: 1818-1889
Physicist

Brooklands Cemetery, Sale, Cheshire. MEM WA North Choir Aisle

JOYCE, James: 1882-1941
Novelist, 'Ulysses'

Fluntern Cemetery, Zurich,
Switzerland

JOYCE, William: 1906-1946 X
'Lord Haw-Haw'

Originally Wandsworth prison
London, moved August 1976 to
Bohermore Cem, Galway, Ireland

KEAN, Edmund: c1787-1833
Actor

St Mary Magdalen, Richmond,
London

KEATS, John: 1795-1821
Poet

Protestant Cemetery, Rome G
MEM WA Poets' Corner

KEBLE, John: 1792-1866
Founder of the Oxford Movement

All Saints', Hursley, Hants.
MEM WA Poets' Corner

KELVIN, 1st Baron
See **Thompson**

KEMBLE, John Philip: 1757-1823
Actor, brother of Sarah Siddons

Lausanne, Switzerland.
Statue WA St Andrew's Chapel

KEPPEL, Admiral Augustus: 1725-1786
1st Viscount

SS Andrew and Patrick, Elveden,
Suffolk

KINGSLEY, Charles: 1819-1875
Poet, Canon of WA

St Mary's, Eversley, Hants YD
MEM St George's Chapel

KIPLING, Rudyard: 1865-1936
Novelist and poet

WA Poets' Corner

KITCHENER, Horatio Herbert: 1850-1916
Field-Marshall, Earl Kitchener of Khartoum

Sunk with HMS Hampshire.
Cenotaph St Paul's Cathedral,
London

KNELLER, Sir Godfrey: 1646-1723
Artist

St Mary-the-Virgin, Twickenham,
Middlesex MEM WA South Choir
Aisle

KNOLLYS, Dame Catherine: c1530-1569
Favourite of Elizabeth I, wife of Francis

WA St Edmund's Chapel

KNOLLYS, Sir Francis: 1514-1596
Treasurer to Elizabeth I

St Nicholas, Rotherfield Greys,
Oxon T

KNOX, John: 1505-1572
Scottish preacher

St Giles, Edinburgh YD

LAMB, Lady Caroline: 1785-1828
Wife of William Lamb

St Etheldreda, Hatfield, Herts

LAMB, Charles: 1775-1834
Essayist

All Saints', Edmonton, London
YD G

LAMB, Mary: 1764-1847
Sister of Charles

As above

LAMB, William: 1779-1848
2nd Viscount Melbourne, 1st PM of
Victoria's reign; PM 1834, 1835-1841

St Etheldreda, Hatfield, Herts

LAMBERT, Daniel: 1770-1809
5 foot 11 inches, weighed 724lb or 53 stones

St Martin's, Stamford, Lincs YD

LANDSEER, Sir Edwin: 1802-1873
Artist and sculptor

St Paul's Cathedral, London

LANGTON, Stephen: c 1150-1228
Divided Old Testament into chapters,
AC 1207-28

Canterbury Cathedral

LAUD, William: 1573-1645 X
AC 1633-1645

Originally All Hallows Barking-by-
the-Tower, reburied in 1663 at
St John's, Oxford

LAW, Andrew Bonar: 1858-1923
PM 1922-1923

WA Nave

LAWRENCE, D H: 1885-1930
(David Herbert) Author

Taos, New Mexico, USA
MEM WA Poets' Corner

LAWRENCE, T E: 1888-1935
(Thomas Edward) 'Lawrence of Arabia'

St Nicholas, Moreton, Dorset YD

LAWRENCE, Sir Thomas: 1769-1830
Artist

St Paul's Cathedral, London

LEAR, Edward: 1812-1888
Artist and nonsense poet

San Remo Cemetery, Italy
MEM WA Poets' Corner

LEE, William: ?-1610
Inventor the stocking frame, 'one of
the most astonishing inventors ever...'

Paris, site unknown

LEGGE, William: 1731-1801
2nd Earl of Dartmouth, founder of
Dartmouth College, New Hampshire, USA

Holy Trinity of the Minoresses,
London D

LELY, St Peter: 1618-1680
Artist

St Paul's Convent Garden, London

LEONARDO DA VINCI: 1452-1519
Artist, sculptor, architect & engineer

St Florentin, Amboise, France

LETHABY, William: 1850-1931
Architect, surveyor of the Abbey fabric

WA West Cloister

LETHBRIDGE, John: 17th century
Inventor of diving machine recovered
£100,000 from wrecks

St Mary the Virgin, Newton
Abbott, Devon YD

LEWIS, C S (Clive Staples): 1898-1963
Theological writer

Holy Trinity, Headington Quarry,
Oxon YD

LEYBOURNE, Sir Roger de: ?-1271
Gave Henry II 40 oaks in 1261
for the Abbey roof

St Peter and St Paul, Leybourne,
Kent. Heart only

LIDDELL, Alice: 1852-1934
Mrs R Hargreaves, the 'Alice' of
'Alice in Wonderland'

St Michael's, Lyndhurst, Hants
YD G

LILBURNE, John: 1614-1657
Political agitator

Moorfields, London YD D

LILLY, William: 1601-1681
Astrologer

St Mary, Walton-on-Thames,
Surrey

LILLYWHITE, (Frederick) William: 1792-1854
Cricketer, introduced round-arm bowling

Highgate Cemetery, London G

LINACRE, Thomas: 1460-1524
Founded Royal College of Physicians

Old St Paul's Cathedral, London D

LIND, Jenny: 1820-1887
Opera singer, 'The Swedish Nightingale'

Great Malvern Cemetery, Worcs
MEM WA Poets' Corner

LINGARD, John: 1771-1851
Priest, wrote only RC History of England
up to his time

St Cuthbert's RC College, Ushaw,
Durham

LINNAEUS, Carl (von Linne): 1707-1778
Botanist

Uppsala Cathedral, Sweden

LISTER, Jospeh: 1827-1912
1st Baron, founder antiseptic surgery

Hampstead Cemetery, London
MEM WA North Choir Aisle

LIVINGSTONE, David: 1813-1873
Explorer

WA Nave, heart at Old Chitambo,
Zambia, Africa

LITTLE JOHN: 13th century
Of Robin Hood legend

St Michael's, Hathersage,
Derbyshire YD G

LLOYD-GEORGE, David: 1863-1945
1st Earl of Dwyfor. PM 1916-1922

Banks of River Dwyfor, Caenarvon,
Gwynedd MEM WA Nave

LOCKE, John: 1632-1704
Philosopher

All Saints, High Laver, Essex T

LOCKYER, Sir Joseph Norman: 1836-1920
Discovered helium and 32
other elements in the sun

St Mary and St Peter's, Salcombe
Regis, Devon YD

LONDON, Jack: 1876-1916
Writer

Glen Ellen, California, USA

LONGESPEE, William: ?-1226
3rd Earl of Salisbury

Salisbury Cathedral T

LONGFELLOW, Henry Wadsworth: 1807-1882
Poet

Cambridge, Mass, USA
MEM WA Poets' Corner

LOVELACE, Richard: 1618-1658
Poet, 'Stone walls do not a prison make...'

St Bride's, Fleet Street, London

LOWE, Sir Hudson: 1769-1844
Governor of St Helena during
Napoleon's imprisonment

St Mark's, North Audley Street,
London

LUTHER, Martin: 1483-1546
Religious reformer

Castle Church, Wittenberg,
Germany

LYELL, Sir Charles: 1797-1875
Founder modern geology

WA Nave, MEM North Aisle

LYTTON, Edward George: 1803-1873
1st Baron Lytton, author 'Last days of Pompeii'

WA St Edmund's Chapel

McADAM, John Loudon: 1756-1836
Road improver

Moffat burial ground, Dumfries
and Galloway

MACAULAY, Thomas Babington: 1800-1859
1st Baron, historian

WA Poets' Corner, MEM

MACDONALD, James Ramsay: 1866-1937
Politician PM 1924, 1929-1935

Spynie, Nr Lossimouth, Grampian,
YD. MEM WA Nave

MACKENZIE, Sir Compton: 1883-1972
Novelist

St Barr, Barra, Western Isles

MACMILLAN, (Maurice) Harold: 1894-1986
1st Earl of Stockton, PM 1957-1963

St Giles, Horsted Keynes, West
Sussex

MALORY, Sir Thomas: ?-1471
Author, 'Morte D'Arthur'

Christ Church, Newgate Street,
London D

MALTHUS, Thomas: 1766-1834
Economist, 'Essay on the Principle of Population'

Bath Abbey

MANNERS, Sir Thomas: ?-1543 1st Earl of Rutland	St Mary's, Bottesford, Leicester T
MANNY, Sir Walter de: ?-1372 Founded Carthusian Monastery that became Charterhouse	Charterhouse, London D
MARLBOROUGH See **Churchill**	
MARLOWE, Christopher: 1564-1582 M Playwright	St Nicholas's, Deptford, London MEM WA Poets' Corner window
MARRYAT, Frederick: 1792-1848 Novelist, 'Mr Midshipman Easy'	St Andrew and St Mary's Langham, Norfolk, YD
MARSHAL, William: c1146-1219 1st Earl of Pembroke	Temple Church, London, effigy
MARTIN, Gregory: ?-1582 Translated Bible into English from the Vulgate – 'Douai version'	St Stephen's, Rheims, France MON
MARVELL, Andrew (the Younger): 1621-1678 Writer	St Giles in the Fields, London MEM
MARX, Karl: 1818-1883 Political philosopher	Highgate Cemetery, London T
MASEFIELD, John: 1878-1967 Poet Laureate	WA Poets' Corner
MASON, William: 1724-1797 Poet	All Saints Aston, South Yorkshire MEM WA Poets' Corner
MAUGHAM, William Somerset: 1874-1965 Novelist	Ashes scattered near King's School, Canterbury
MAYHEW, Henry: 1812-1887 Founder of Punch Magazine and social reformer	Kensal Green Cemetery, London
MELBOURNE, Lord See **Lamb, William**	
MENDELSSOHN, Felix: 1809-1847 Composer	Alter Dreifaltigkeits Kirchhof, Berlin
MENZIES, Sir Robert: 1894-1978 Australian Prime Minister	Prime Ministers' Memorial Garden, Melbourne Central Cemetery, Adelaide, South Australia

MEREDITH, George: 1828-1909
Novelist and poet

Dorking Cemetery, Surrey

MERTON, Walter de: ?-1277
Founder of Merton College, Oxford

Rochester Cathedral T

MICHELANGELO: 1475-1564
(di Lodovico Buonarroti Simoni)
Sculptor, painter and poet

Santa Croce, Florence T

MILDMAY, Thomas: ?-1544
Received surrender of monasteries
in East Anglia

Chelmsford Cathedral with 41
other Mildmays from 1544 to
1798

MILDMAY, Sir Walter: 1520-1589
Chancellor of the Exchequer to Elizabeth 1

St Bartholomew the Great,
London T

MILL, James: 1773-1836
Father of John Stuart, utilitarian

St Mary Abbots, Kensington,
London

MILL, John Stuart: 1806-1873
Philosopher

St Veran Cemetery, Avignon,
France

MILLAIS, Sir John Everett: 1829-1896
Artist

St Paul's Cathedral, London B

MILLAR, Joe: 1684-1738
Comedian - jokes still used

Portugal Street Cemetery,
London D

MILLER, William: 1795-1861
Helped liberate Chile and Peru

Pantheon, Lima, Peru

MILLS, John: ?-1811
Last survivor of 'Black Hole of Calcutta'

Old St Pancras, London YD D

MILTON, John: 1608-1674
Poet

St Giles Cripplegate, London
MEM WA Poets' Corner

MILTON, Katherine: ?-1658
2nd wife of John Milton

St Margaret's, London, YD

MONCK, General George: 1608-1670
1st Duke of Albemarle, soldier

WA Henry VII Chapel north aisle
MEM Henry VII Chapel south aisle

MONTFORT, Simon de: 1208-1265 K
Earl of Leicester

Benedictine Abbey, Evesham,
Worcs T D (head, one foot, both
hands buried elsewhere)

MONTGOMERY, Field Marshal: 1887-1976
(Bernard Law) 1st Viscount Montgomery of
Alamein: soldier

Holy Cross, Binsted, Hants YD

MOORE, Henry: 1898-1986
Sculptor

Perry Green, Herts. MEM St Paul's
Cathedral Crypt

MORE, Sir Thomas (Saint): 1478-1535 X
Martyr and politician

St Peter-ad-Vincula, Tower of
London or Possibly in Chelsea Old
Church, body only.
Head in St Dunstan's, Canterbury

MORLAND, Sir Samuel: 1625-1695
Inventor, worked for Cromwell and Charles II

St Paul's, Hammersmith, London.
Monuments of two wives in WA
Nave

MORRIS, William: 1834-1896
Poet, socialist, designer.

St George's, Kelmscott, Oxon YD

MORRISON, Jim: 1943-1971
Lead singer 'The Doors'

Père Lachaise Cemetery, Paris

MORTIMER, Roger: c1286-1330 X
Lover of Edward III's mother

Greyfriars, Newgate, London D

MORTIMER, Roger, of Usk: 1374-1398
Named by Richard II as heir to the throne

Wigmore Abbey, Herefordshire D

MOUNTBATTEN, Lord Louis: 1900-1979 M
1st Earl Mountbatten of Burma

Romsey Abbey, Hants
MEM WA Nave

MOWBRAY, Anne
See **Royal section**

MOZART, Wolfgang Amadeus: 1756-1791
Composer

St Mary, Vienna, in common grace
with 20 paupers, MON erected
1869

MURRAY, Gilbert: 1866-1957
Classical scholar

WA Poets' Corner

MYDDLETON, Sir Hugh: 1560-1631
Brought New River to London for
drinking purposes

St Matthew's, Friday Street,
London D

NAPIER, Robert: 1810-1890
1st Baron of Magdala, Field Marshal

St Paul's Cathedral, London

NASH, Richard 'Beau': 1674-1762
Dandy

Bath Abbey

NELSON, Catherine: 1767-1842
(Mrs Matcham) Sister of Lord Nelson

St Mary, Slaugham, West Sussex
YD

NELSON, Frances: 1761-1831
Wife of Lord Nelson

St Margaret and St Andrew,
Littleham, Devon YD

NELSON, Horatia: 1801-1881
Daughter of Horatio by Lady Hamilton

Paines Lanes cemetery, Pinner, Middlesex YD G

NELSON, Admiral Horatio: 1758-1805 K
1st Viscount

St Paul's Cathedral, London T
Buried in Cardinal Wolsey's sarcophagus

NEVILL, Ralph: 1346-1425
1st Earl of Westmorland: 2nd wife, Joan Beaufort grandmother of Edward IV

St Gregory, Staindrop, Durham T
with effigy of 2 wives

NEVILL, Richard: 1400-1460
Earl of Salisbury, father of the 'Kingmaker'

Bisham Abbey, Berks D

NEVILL, Richard: 1428-1471 K
Earl of Warwick, 'The Kingmaker'

Bisham Abbey, Berks D

NEWMAN, John Henry: 1801-1890
Cardinal

Rednal (Oratory Fathers)
Warwickshire YD

NEWTON, Sir Isaac: 1642-1727
Astrologer, inventor of calculus

WA Nave, MEM Choir Screen

NEWTON, Revd John: 1725-1807
Hymn writer

Originally St Mary Woolnoth, London, transferred 1893 to St Peter and St Paul, Olney, Bucks YD T

NICHOLLS, Colonel Richard: 1625-1672 K
Captured New York from Dutch and named it after James II, Duke of York

St Andrew's Ampthill, Beds, MEM with cannonball which killed him

NICHOLLS, Sir Frances: ?-1621
Governor at Tilbury when Elizabeth made Armada speech

St Leonard, Hardwick, Northants MON

NIGHTINGALE, Florence: 1820-1910
Nurse and hospital reformer

St Margaret's, East Wellow, Hants YD. MEM St Paul's Cathedral, London

NIJINSKY, Vaslav: 1890-1950
Dancer

Montparnasse Cemetery, Paris

NOONAN, Robert P: 1870-1911
Author 'Ragged Trousered Philanthropists' under pen name Robert Tressell

Walton Park Cemetery, Lancs

NORRIS, Henry: c1525-1601
1st Baron: statesman

St Michael and All Angels, Rycote, Oxon MEM WA Chapel of St Andrew

NORRIS, Margaret: ?-1599
Wife of Henry

As **Norris Henry**

NORTH, Lord Frederick: 1732-1792
2nd Earl of Guildford:
PM 1770-1782 (during American Revolution)

All Saints', Wroxton, Oxon T

NOVELLO, Ivor: 1893-1951
Composer, singer, actor

Golders Green, London
MEM St Paul's Cathedral, London

NOYE, (or NOY) William: 1577-1634
Attorney-general to Charles I

St Lawrence's, Brentford,
Middlesex

OCKHAM, (or OCCAM) William: c1285-1349
Philosopher 'Occam's razor'

Franciscan Monastery, Munich

ODO: c1036- 1097
Half-brother of William the Conqueror

Palermo, Italy T

OGLETHORPE, General James: 1696-1785
Founder of Georgia USA

All Saints, Cranham, Essex MON

OGLETHORPE, Owen: ?-1559
Bishop of Carlisle, crowned Elizabeth I

St Dunstan in the West, London D

OLIVIER, Laurence: 1907-1989
Baron Olivier, actor

WA Poets' Corner

ORWELL, George
See **Blair, Eric**

OUGHTRED, William: c1573-1660
Invented the X for multiplication and
the :: for proportion

Old Church of St Peter and St
Paul, Albury, Surrey

OWEN, Robert: 1771-1858
Social reformer, founder of the
co-operative movement

Kensal Green Cemetery, London

PANKHURST, Emmeline: 1858-1928
Women's liberation suffragette

Brompton Cemetery, London

PAOLI, General Pasquale de: 1725-1807
Liberated Corsica

Originally in old RC Cemetery, St
Pancras, moved to Corsica. Bust
WA South Choir Aisle

PARKER, Archbishop Matthew: 1504-1575
'Nosey Parker' AC 1559-1575

Sanctuary, Lambeth Palace Chapel,
London

PARNELL, Charles Stewart: 1846-1891
Irish politician

Glasnevin Cemetery, Dublin

PARNELL, Thomas: 1679-1718
Poet, friend of Addison and Steele

Holy Trinity, Chester, Cheshire

PARR, Thomas: 1483-1635
Supposed to have lived 152 years

WA Poets' Corner

PARR, Lord William: 1434-1483
Uncle of Catherine Parr

St Mary's, Horton, Northants T

PASTON, John: 1421-1466
Paston letters

Originally in Priory Church,
Bromholm, Norfolk, possibly
removed to Paston at Dissolution

PAULINUS, Saint: ?-644
Apostle to Northumbria

Rochester Cathedral crypt, site
unknown

PEABODY, George: 1795-1869
Peabody Trust, operates 16,000
flats in and around London

Body lay in WA then taken to
South Danvers, Mass, USA.
MEM WA Nave

PEARS, Sir Peter: 1910-1986
Singer

St Peter and St Paul, Aldeburgh,
Suffolk YD

PEEL, John: 1776-1854
Hunstman, subject of the song

St Kentigern's, Caldbeck,
Cumbria T

PEEL, Sir Robert: 1788-1850
1829 created modern police force
PM 1834, 1841-1846

St Peter's, Drayton Bassett, Staff.
Statue WA North Transept

PELHAM, Sir John: 14th century
Captured King John of France at battle of Poitiers

Saleshurst Abbey, Sussex D

PEMBROKE, Aymer de Valence: c1270-1324
Earl of Pembroke: cousin to Edward I

WA Sanctuary T

PEMBROKE, Mary de St Pol: 1304-1377
Countess of Pembroke, wife of Aymer,
foundress of Pembroke College, Cambridge

Denny Abbey, Cambridgeshire D
MEM WA North Ambulatory

PENDERELL, Richard: ?-1672
Helped Charles II escape after
battle of Worcester

St Giles in the Fields, London

PENN, Admiral Sir William: 1621-1670
Father of William Penn

St Mary Redcliffe, Bristol G

PENN, William: 1644-1718
Founder of Pennsylvania USA

Jordans, Chalfont St. Giles,
Bucks G

PENTREATH, Dolly: 1685-1777
Last person to speak Cornish as a
native language

Paul Parish yard, Cornwall plaque
given by Prince Louis Lucien
Bonaparte, 1860

PEPYS, Samuel: 1633-1703
Diarist

St Olave's, Hart Street, London, modern MON

PERCEVAL, Spencer: 1762-1812 M
PM 1809-1812
Only British Prime Minister assassinated

St Luke, Charlton, London
MEM WA Nave

PERCY, Sir Henry: 1364-1403 K
Hotspur

St Alkmund's, Whitchurch, Salop.
Exhumed soon after, decapitated and quartered

PERCY, Sir Henry: 1502-1537 X
6th Earl of Northumberland

St John's, Hackney, London D

PERKIN, Sir William: 1838-1907
Discovered aniline dyes

Sudbury, Brent, London, YD

PERROT, Sir John: 1527-1592
Illegitimate son of Henry VIII

St Peter-ad-Vincula, Tower of London Not executed

PHILIPS, John: 1676-1708
Poet

Hereford Cathedral,
MEM WA Poets' Corner

PHILLIP, Captain Arthur: 1738-1814
1st Governor New South Wales

St Nicholas, Bathampton, Somerset G

PIAF, Edith: 1915-1963
Singer

Père Lachaise Cemetery, Paris

PICKERING, Sir William: 1516-1575
Elizabeth I's ambassador to France

St Helen's, Bishopsgate, London T

PIERPOINT, Simon de: 12th century
With Richard I at the siege of Acre

Holy Trinity, Hurstpierpoint,

PITT, William: 1708-1778
1st Earl of Chatham, 'The Great Commoner'
PM 1756-1761, 1766-1768

WA North Transept, MON

PITT, William: 1759-1806
'The Younger'. Aged 24 PM 1783-1801
and 1804-1806

WA in father's grave,
statue over great west door

PIZARRO, Francisco: c1478-1541
Destroyed the Inca Empire

Lima, Peru

POCAHONTAS: 1595-1617
Native American, married John Rolfe

St George's, Gravesend, Kent D

POE, Edgar Allan: 1809-1849
American writer

Westminster Presbyterian Church, Baltimore, Md, USA

POLE, Sir Geoffrey: 1502-1558
Brother of the Cardinal, imprisoned
by Henry VIII but died natural death

Stoughton, West Sussex

POLE, Reginald: 1500-1558
Last RC AC1556-1558

Canterbury Cathedral

POLE, William de la: 1396-1450 X
1st Duke of Suffolk, husband of Alice Chaucer

St Andrew's, Wingfield, Suffolk T

POPE, Alexander: 1688-1744
Poet

St Mary the Virgin, Twickenham,
London, MEM WA Poet's Corner

POTTER, (Helen) Beatrix: 1866-1943
children's author and illustrator

Ashes scattered on the Cumbrian
Fells

POWELL, Foster: 1731-1793
Britain's first athlete,
walked 400 miles in 135 hours

Chapel of St Faith in St Paul's
Cathedral, YD D

PRIESTLEY, J B: 1894-1984
(John Boynton) Writer

St Michael and All Angels,
Hubberholme, North Yorkshire

PRIESTLEY, Joseph: 1733-1804
Chemist, discovered oxygen

Northumberland, Pa, USA

PRIOR, Matthew: 1664-1721
Poet

WA Poet's Corner, bust

PRYNNE, William: 1600-1669
Pamphleteer and publisher

In walk under Lincoln's Inn
Chapel, London

PUGIN, Augustus Welby: 1812-1852
With Barry, architect of Parliament buildings

Pugin Chantry, St Augustine's
RC Church, Ramsgate, Kent T

PURCELL, Henry: c1658-1695
Composer

WA North Choir aisle

QUEENSBURY, 8th Marquess
see **Douglas, Sir John Sholto**

QUILLER-COUCH,
Sir Arthur Thomas: 1863-1944
Man of letters

St Nicholas's, Fowey, Cornwall
MON

R-101 VICTIMS: 1930
Crashed Beauvais, France

St Mary's, Cardington, Beds, YD

RAFFLES, Sir Thomas Stamford: 1781-1826
Founder of Singapore and Zoological Society

St Mary's Hendon, London
MEM WA North Choir Aisle

RAGLAN, James Henry Somerset: 1788-1855
Baron, Lord Fitzroy Charge of the Light Brigade.
Raglan sleeve

St Michael and All Angels,
Badminton, Glos

RAHERE: 1080-1145
Founder of St Bartholomew's church
and hospital

St Bartholomew the Great,
London, 15th century T

RAIKES, Robert: 1735-1811
Founder of Sunday Schools

St Mary's, Gloucester

RALEIGH, Carew: 1605-1666
Son of Walter Raleigh

St Margaret's, Westminster Abbey,
London

RALEIGH, Sir Walter: 1552-1618 X
Courtier, navigator and poet

St Margaret's, Westminster Abbey,
London. Head in West Horsley,
Surrey

RECORDE, Robert: 1510-1558
Invented the equal sign & introduced
the plus & minus signs from Germany

Died Southwark prison

RENNIE, John: 1761-1821
Engineer & designer of
old Waterloo and London bridges

St Paul's Cathedral, London

REYNOLDS, Sir Joshua: 1723-1792
Artist

St Paul's Cathedral, London

RHODES, Cecil: 1853-1902
Rhodesia named after him
also Rhodes Scholarship

Matoppo Hills, Zimbabwe
MEM WA Henry VII Chapel
south side

RICH, Saint Edmund: 1180-1240
AC 1234-1240

Pontigny, France

RICH, Lord Richard: 1486-1567
Lord Chancellor, betrayed More & Fisher,
manoeuvred Thomas Cromwell's fall

Holy Cross, Felsted, Essex T

RICHARDSON, Samuel: 1689-1761
'Father of the English novel'

St Bride's, London

RICHELIEU Cardinal, Duc de: 1585-1642
Armand Jean du Plessis

Chapel of Sorbonne, Paris.
Tomb rifled at Revolution

RIZZIO, David: 1533-1566 M
Secretary to Mary Queen of Scots

Probably Holyrood Abbey

ROBIN HOOD: 13th century
Legendary outlaw

Kirklees Abbey, Mirfield, Yorks G

ROBSART, Amy: 1532-1560
Wife of Robert Dudley

St Mary the Virgin, Oxford MEM

ROGET, Dr Peter Mark: 1779-1869
Creator of 'Roget's Thesaurus'

St James's, West Malvern, Worcs

ROLLE, Richard de Hampole: 1290-1349
Hermit and author

Hampole, West Yorkshire

ROLLS, Charles Stewart: 1877-1910
1st Englishman killed in a plane
Joint founder of Rolls-Royce

St Cadoc, Llangattock-Vibon-Avel,
Gwent, YD

ROMNEY, George: 1734-1802
Artist

St Mary's, Dalton-in-Furness,
Lancs, YD

ROPER, Margaret: 1505-1544
Daughter of Sir Thomas More

St Dunstain's, Canterbury

ROSAMUND, CLIFFORD: ?-1176
'Fair Rosamond', Mistress of Henry II

Godstow, Oxon ruins

ROSSETTI, Christina Georgina: 1830-1894
Poet, sister of Dante Gabriel Rossetti

Highgate Cemetery, London

ROSSETTI, Dante Gabriel: 1828-1882
Poet

All Saints', Birchington, Kent YD

ROTHSCHILD, Nathan Meyer: 1777-1836
Financier

Jewish Burial Ground, Brady
Street, Whitechapel, London

ROTHSCHILD, Nathan: 1840-1915
1st Baron, financier and benefactor

United Synagogue Cemetery,
Willesden, London

ROUBILIAC, Louis François: c1705-1762
Sculptor

St Martin in the Fields, London D

ROUSSEAU, Jean Jacques: 1712-1778
Philosopher

Pantheon, Paris.
Body stolen 1814

ROWE, Nicholas: 1674-1718
Poet Laureate

WA Poets' Corner, MEM now in
Triforium

ROYCE, Sir Henry Bt: 1863-1933
Joint founder of Rolls Royce

St Andrew, Alwalton Hunts
MEM WA Nave window

RUBENS, Sir Peter Paul: 1577-1640
Artist

St Jacques's, Antwerp, Belgium

RUSKIN, John: 1819-1900
Author and art critic

St Andrew's, Coniston, Cumbria,
YD. MEM WA Poets' Corner

RUSSELL, George William: 1867-1935
Pseudonym 'AE') Poet & artist

Mount Jerome Cemetery, Dublin

RUTHERFORD, Ernest: 1871-1937
1st Baron Rutherford, physicist

WA Nave

RYMER, Thomas: 1641-1713
Compiler of 'Foedera'

St Clement Danes, London

RYSBRACK, John Michael: 1694-1770
Sculptor

Marylebone, London YD D

SACKVILLES of Dorset: 1694-1770
5th & 6th Earl, 3rd & 4th Duke & 3rd Duchess

St Michael, Withyham, East Sussex

SADLER, Sir Ralph: 1507-1587
Diplomat

St Mary, Standon, Herts T

SARGEANT, Sir Malcolm: 1895-1967
Conductor

Stamford Cemetery, Lincs

SASSOON, Siegfried: 1886-1967
Poet, novelist

Downside Abbey, Somerset
MEM WA Poets' Corner

SAYERS, Thomas: 1826-1865
Pugilist, beaten once & only after 61 rounds

Highgate Cemetery, London

SCHEEMAKERS, Peter: 1691-1770
Sculptor. 12 monuments in Westminster Abbey

Antwerp, Belgium

SCHEEMAKERS, Thomas: 1740-1808
Sculptor

St Pancras Old Church, London D

SCHOMBERG, Frederick: 1615-1690
1st Duke of Schomberg

St Patrick's Cathedral, Dublin

SCOTT, Sir George Gilbert: 1811-1878
Architect

WA Nave

SCOTT, Captain Robert Falcon: 1868-1912
Antarctic explorer

Antarctica

SCOTT, Sir Walter: 1771-1832
Novelist and poet

Dryburgh Abbey, Roxburgh,
Scotland MEM WA Poets' Corner.
MEM window in Church of
Scotland, Covent Garden, London

SEDBURGH, Adam: ?-1537 X
Abbot of Jervaulx, took part in
Pilgrimage of Grace

Cloister, Jervaulx Abbey ruins,
North Yorkshire, D

SELDEN, John: 1584-1654
Jurist, oriental scholar, historical & legal books,
his books in the Bodleian Library, Oxford

Temple Church, London

SEWELL, Anna: 1820-1878
Novelist, 'Black Beauty'

Friends burial ground, Lemas,
Norfolk

SEYMOUR, Edward: 1506-1552 X
1st Earl of Hertford, Duke of Somerset,
Protector, brother of Jane,

St Peter-ad-Vincula, Tower of
London

SEYMOUR, Lord Edward: ?-1574
One of 3 sons of the Protector, all of whom were
named Edward & this one married 3 times
& 2 of his wives were named Frances Howard

St Mary, Berry Pomeroy, Devon T

SEYMOUR, Lord Edward: 1539-1621
2nd Earl of Hertford

Salisbury Cathedral T

SEYMOUR, Frances: 1554-1598
Frances Howard of Effingham,
Countess of Hertford

WA St Benedict's Chapel

SEYMOUR, Frances: ?-1639
France Howard of Bindon,
Duchess of Richmond & Lennox

WA Henry VII Chapel

SEYMOUR, Baron Thomas: 1508-1549 X
Married Catherine Parr after death of
Henry VIII

St Peter-ad-Vincula, Tower of
London

SHACKLETON, Sir Ernest: 1874-1922
Explorer

Grytviken, S. Georgia, Falkland
Islands

SHADWELL, Thomas: 1642-1692
Poet Laureate

Chelsea Old Church, London YD
MEM WA Poets' Corner

SHAKESPEARE, Edmund: 1580-1607
Youngest brother of William

Southwark Cathedral, site
unknown, memorial plaque

SHAKESPEARE, William: 1564-1616
Playwright

Holy Trinity, Stratford-upon-Avon,
Warks G (grave 17 feet deep).
MEM WA Poets' Corner

SHARP, Granville: 1735-1813
Philanthropist, anti-slavery

All Saints', Fulham, London YD.
MEM WA Poets' Corner

SHAW, George Bernard: 1856-1950
Dramatist, essayist, critic and pamphleteer

Ayot St Lawrence, Herts,
ashes scattered in the gardens

SHAW, (Richard) Norman: 1831-1912
Architect designed Old Scotland Yard

St John's, Hampstead, London

SHELLEY, Mary Wollstonecraft: 1797-1851
Author 'Frankenstein'

St Peter's, Bournemouth, Dorset
Body removed to here from
St Pancras Churchyard 1851

SHELLEY, Percy Bysshe: 1792-1822
Poet

Drowned, body burned on beach,
ashes in Rome Protestant
Cemetery, heart St Peter's,
Bournemouth
MEM WA Poets' Corner

SHERIDAN, Richard Brinsley: 1751-1816
Dramatist, 'The Rivals'

WA Poets' Corner

SHIELD, William: 1748-1829
Master of the King's Music

WA South Cloister

SHILLIBEER, George: 1797-1866
Introduced the omnibus & word into England

St Mary the Virgin, Chigwell,
Essex B

SHIRLEY, James: 1596-1666
Dramatist, poet

St Giles in the Fields, London

SHOVELL, Admiral Sir Cloudesly: 1650-1707 M
Assisted in capture of Gibraltar

WA South Choir Aisle MEM

SHREWSBURY: see **Bess of Hardwick**

SIDDONS, Sarah: 1755-1831
Actress

St Mary's, Paddington Green,
London YD
MEM WA St Andrew's Chapel

SIDNEY, Algernon: 1622-1683 X
Politician

St John the Baptist, Penshurst,
Kent

SIDNEY, Frances: 1583-1612
Countess of Rutland, daughter of Philip

St Leonard's, Shoreditch,
London D

SIDNEY, Mary: see **Herbert, Mary**

SIDNEY, Sir Philip: 1554-1586
Poet, statesman, soldier

Old St Paul's Cathedral, London,
buried in Crypt, coffin seen after
Great Fire

SIMCOE, Lt Gen John Graves: 1752-1806
Founded Toronto

Wolford Chapel, Nr Dunkeswell,
Devon

SIMON of SUDBURY: ?-1381 M
AC 1375-1381

Canterbury Cathedral. Beheaded
by rioters, head in St Gregory,
Sudbury, Suffolk
(replaced by cannon ball)

SITWELL, Dame Edith: 1887-1964
Poet, writer, publisher

St Mary's, Weedon Lois,
Northants, YD

SKELTON, John: 1460-1529
Earliest known Poet Laureate

St Margaret's, WA, London YD

SLOANE, Sir Hans: 1660-1753
His collection of antiquities became
foundation of British Museum

Chelsea Old Church YD T

SMEATON, John: 1724-1794
Designed 3rd Eddystone lighthouse

St Mary, Whitkirk, West Yorkshire
MEM WA Nave

SMITH, Adam: 1723-1790
Economist

Canongate Church, Edinburgh, YD

SMITH, George: 1824-1901
Philanthropic publisher, founder
Dictionary of National Biography

St Mary, Byfleet, Surrey YD

SMITH, Captain John: 1580-1631
Life saved by Pochahontas

St Sepulchre, Holborn, London G
MEM window in church

SMITH, Thomas: ?-1699
Founder of modern banking

St Mary's, Nottingham

SMITH, W H (William Henry): 1825-1891
Newsagents, bookstores

Hambledon Cemetery, Bucks

SMITHSON, James: 1765-1829
Founder of Smithsonian Museum
in Washington, USA

Washington, DC, USA

SMYTH, Charles Piazzi: 1819-1900
Astronomer, studied Great Pyramid
from which he deduced the end of
the world being 1882

Sharrow, Ripon, North Yorkshire
YD

SNACHENBERG, Helen: ?-1565
Marchioness of Northampton,
Maid of honour to Elizabeth

Salisbury Cathedral T

SOANE, Sir John: 1753-1837
Architect

St Pancras Old Church, London YD

SOMERS, Admiral Sir George: 1554-1610
Colonised Bermuda

St Candida and Holy Cross,
Whitchurch Canonicorum,
Dorset G

SOMERS, William: ?-1560
Henry VIII's fool

St Leonard's, Shoreditch,
London D

SOUTHNEY, Robert: 1774-1843
Poet, 'Battle of Blenheim'

St Kentigern's, Crosswaite,
Cumbria, YD.
MEM WA Poets' Corner

SOUTHWORTH, Saint John: 1592-1654 X
Cromwell martyr

Hanged, drawn & quartered at
Tyburn, brought to Westminster
Cathedral, London in 1930

SPEED, John: 1542-1629
Historian and cartographer

St Giles Cripplegate, London D

SPENCE, Joseph: 1699-1768
'Anecdotes'

St Mary, Byfleet, Surrey YD

SPENSER, Edmund: 1552-1599
Elizabethan poet

WA Poets' Corner, site unknown

SPRING, Howard: 1889-1965
Novelist

St Mylor's, Cornwall, YD

STANHOPE, Earls of: 1673-1967
1st, 2nd, 3rd, 6th, 7th (and last)

St Botolph, Chevening, Kent
MEM WA Choir Screen

STANHOPE, Philip: 1732-1768
Illegitimate son of 4th Earl of Chesterfield

St Peter, Limpsfield, Surrey
(& his wife, Eugenia, who sold
the famous letters)

STANLEY, Dean Arthur Penrhyn: 1815-1881

WA Henry VII Chapel T

STANLEY, Sir Henry Morton: 1841-1904
Explorer, found Livingstone

St Michael and All Angels,
Pirbright, Surrey YD

STEELE, Sir Richard: 1672-1729
Edited 'The Tatler'

St Peter's, Carmarthen, Wales

STEPHENSON, George: 1781-1848
Railway builder

Holy Trinity, Chesterfield,
Derbyshire. MEM window WA
North Choir Aisle

STEPHENSON, Robert: 1803-1859
Bridge Builder

WA Nave B. MEM window WA
North Choir Aisle

STERNE, Laurence: 1713-1768
Author 'Tristram Shandy'

Originally buried in London but
body stolen for medical use; on
being recognised, it was returned
to grave; removed in 1969 to
St Michael's, Coxwold, Yorkshire
YD G

STEVENSON, Robert Louis: 1850-1894
Author 'Treasure Island'

Mount Veam, Samoa

STOW, John: 1525-1605
Chronicler 'Survey of London'

St Andrew Undershaft, London T

STRAFFORD, Thomas Wentworth: 1593-1641 X
1st Earl of

St John the Baptist, Hooton
Roberts, Yorkshire, with wife and
daughter; MON at Wentworth

STREET, George Edmund: 1824-1881
Architectural pupil of George Gilbert Scott,
designed London Law Courts

WA Nave B

STRICKLAND, Agnes: 1796-1874
Author, 'Lives of the Queens'

St Edmund, King & Martyr,
Southwold, Suffolk, YD

STRICKLAND, Elizabeth: 1794-1875
Co-author with above

All Saints', Tilford, Surrey YD

STRYPE, John: 1643-1737
Historian

Leyton, Sussex

STUBBS, George: 1724-1806
Painter, particularly of horses

St Marylebone, London D

SUCKLING, Sir John: 1609-1642
Poet, invented cribbage

Protestant Cemetery, Paris

SULLIVAN, Sir Arthur: 1842-1900
Composer, (Gilbert and ...)

St Paul's Cathedral, London

SUTTON, Thomas: 1552-1611
Refounded Charterhouse School (see Manny)

Charterhouse, London T.
Viscera, Hackney

SWEDENBORG, Emanuel: 1688-1772
Scientist

Originally London, moved 1908
Uppsala, Sweden

SWIFT, Jonathan: 1667-1745
Satirist, 'Gulliver's Travels'

St Patrick's Cathedral, Dublin

SWINBURNE, Algernon Charles: 1837-1909
Poet and critic

St Boniface, Bonchurch,
Isle of Wight

SYMINGTON, William: 1763-1831
Steamship pioneer

St Botolph's, Aldgate, London YD

TALBOT, Elizabeth:
See **Bess of Hardwick**

TALLIS, Thomas: 1505-1585
Father of English Church music

St Alphege, Greenwich, London

TATE, Sir Henry: 1819-1899
Sugar Magnate & philanthropist,
hospitals & Tate gallery

Norwood Cemetery, London

TAUBER, Richard: 1891-1948
Opera singer

Brompton Cemetery, London

TAYLOR, Edmund Seyfung: 1854-1908
Founder Rambling Clubs, wrote as 'Walker Miles',

Godstone, Surrey,
MEM Leith Hill, Surrey

TELFORD, Thomas: 1757-1834
Civil engineer, Menai Bridge

WA Nave, MEM WA
St Andrew's Chapel

TEMPEST, Sir Richard: ?-1488

St Alkenda's, Giggleswick,
Yorhshire T. Buried with the head
of his favourite horse

TENNYSON, Alfred, Lord: 1809-1892
Poet Laureate

WA Poets' Corner

TENNYSON, Lady Emily: 1813-1896
Wife of poet

All Saints', Freshwater,
Isle of Wight YD

TERRY, Dame Ellen: 1848-1928
Actress

St Paul's, Covent Garden, London

THACKERAY, William Makepeace: 1811-1863
Author

Kensal Green Cemetery, London
MEM WA Poets' Corner

THEODORE, Etienne: 1686-1756
King of Corsica

St Anne's, Soho, London D

THOMAS, Dylan: 1914-1953
Poet

Laugharne, Wales, YD
MEM WA Poets' corner

THOMSON, James: 1700-1748
Poet

St Mary Magdelen, Richmond,
Surrey, MEM WA Poets' Corner

THOMSON, William: 1824-1907
1st Baron Kelvin, scientist, inventor

WA Nave, MEM WA Nave window

THORNDIKE, Dame Sybil: 1882-1976
Actress

WA South Choir Aisle

THORNHILL, Sir James: 1675-1734
Designed Great West & North Transept
windows of WA

St James's, Finsbury, London

THROCKMORTON, Sir Nicholas: 1515-1571
Ambassador to France and Scotland

St Katherine Cree, London D

THURLOE, John: 1616-1668
Secretary of State under Olive Cromwell

Lincoln's Inn Chapel, London

TIPTOFT, John: 1427-1470 X
Earl of Worcester, the 'Butcher of England',
he executed 20 Lancastrians by impalement

St Ann's, Blackfriars, D
MON Ely Cathedral

TIZARD, Sir Henry: 1885-1959
Scientist – radar

Oriel College, Oxford

TOLKEIN, J R R: 1892-1973
(John Ronald Reuel) Author 'Lord of the Rings'

Wolvercote Cemetery , Oxford

TOMPION, Thomas: 1638-1713
'Finest clockmaker of all time'

WA Nave

TOPLADY, Augustus: 1740-1778
Hymnist 'Rock of Ages'

Tottenham Court Road Chapel,
London D

TRADESCANT, John: 1570-1637
Traveller and gardener

St Mary's Lambeth, London YD,
also his son and grandson

TREE, Sir Herbert Beerbohm: 1853-1917
Actor manager

St John's, Hampstead, London YD

TRENCHARD, Hugh Montague: 1873-1956
1st Viscount Trenchard, founder of the RAF

WA Henry VII Chapel

TRESSELL, Robert: see **Noonan, Robert**

TREVITHICK, Richard: 1771-1833
Invented locomotive engine,
screw propulsion for ships

St Edmund's, Dartford, Kent D
MEM WA under NW tower

TROLLOPE, Anthony: 1815-1882
Author, introduced the pillar box

Kensal Green Cemetery, London
MEM WA Poets' Corner

TRYON, William: 1725-1788
1st English governor of New York City

St Mary's, Twickenham, London
YD

TUDOR, Edward: ?-1472
Uncle of Henry VII & monk at Westminster

WA Poets' Corner

TUDOR, Edmund: 1430-1456
Earl of Richmond, husband of Margaret Beaufort,
father of Henry VII

St David's Cathedral,
Pembrokeshire

TUDOR, Owen: ?-1461 X
Husband of Catherine of Valois
& grandfather to Henry VII

Greyfriars, Hereford D

TUNSTALL, Cuthbert: 1474-1559
Bishop of London & Durham

Lambeth Palace, London

TURNER, Anne: 1576-1615 X
Hanged at Tyburn for helping the
Countess of Essex poison
Sir Thomas Overbury

St Martin in the Fields,
London, Cemetery D

TURNER, J M W: 1775-1851
(Joseph, Mallord, William) Artist

St Paul's Cathedral, London

TURPIN, Richard (Dick): 1706-1749 X
Highwayman

St George's, York YD

TYNDALE, William: c1494-1536 X
Translated Bible into English

Burnt at Vilvorde, Nr Brussels,
Belgium MEM WA South Choir
Aisle

USSHER, Archbishop James: 1581-1656
Discovered from the Bible that world began 4004 BC

WA St Paul's Chapel

VALENCE, William de: ?-1296
Lord of Pembroke & Wexford, father of Aymer,
half-brother of Henry III

WA St Edmund's Chapel T

VALETTE, Jean Parisot de la: 1494-1568
Leader of the Knights of St John at the
siege of Malta

Valetta, Malta

VANBRUGH, Sir John: 1664-1726
Playwright & architect, Blenheim Palace

St Stephen Walbrook, London

VANCOUVER, Captain George: 1757-1798
Explorer of the North American coast

St Peter's, Petersham, Richmond,
London YD

VAN DYCK, Sir Anthony: 1599-1641
Artist

Old St Paul's Cathedral, London D
MEM in crypt

VAUGHAN WILLIAMS, Ralph: 1872-1958
Composer

WA North Choir Aisle

VERNEY, Sir Edmund: ?-1642
Standard bearer to Charles I

All Saints, Middle Claydon,
Bucks T

VERNON, Admiral Edward: 1684-1757
'Old Grog'

St Martin, Nacton, Suffolk
MEM WA North Transept

VILLENEUVE, Pierre de: 1763-1806
French Admiral at Trafalgar

Rennes, France

VILLIERS, Barbara: 1641-1709
Duchess of Cleveland, bore 5 illegitimate
children to Charles II

St Nicholas, Chiswick, London

VILLIERS, George: 1592-1628
1st Duke of Buckingham

WA Henry VII Chapel

VOLTAIRE: 1694-1778
Pen name of François- Marie Arouet

Pantheon, Paris, remains stolen
1814, heart returned in 1864

WALBROOK, Anton: 1900-1967
Actor

St John's, Hampstead, London YD

WALLACE, Alfred Russel: 1823-1913
Joint paper with Darwin in 1858
about evolution

Broadstone Cemetery, Dorset.
MEM WA North Choir Aisle

WALLACE, Edgar: 1875-1932
Author, mystery stories

Little Marlow Cemetery, Bucks

WALPOLE, Horace: 1717-1797
4th Earl of Orford, man of letters

St Martin, Houghton, Norfolk

WALPOLE, Sir Hugh: 1884-1941
Novelist

Keswick, Cumbria YD

WALPOLE, Sir Robert: 1676-1745
1st Earl of Orford, 1st PM 1721-1742

St Martin, Houghton, Norfolk

WALSINGHAM, Sir Francis: 1530-1590
Headed Elizabeth I's Secret Service

Old St Paul's Cathedral, London D

WALTHEOF: ?-1076 X
Husband of William the Conqueror's
niece, only man executed by him

Croyland Abbey ruins, Lincs,

WALTON, Brian: 1600-1661
Wrote Polygot Bible

Old St Paul's Cathedral, London D

WALTON, Izaak: 1593-1683
Author 'The Compleat Angler'

Winchester Cathedral G

WALTON, Sir William: 1902-1983
Composer

Italy, MEM WA North Choir Aisle

WALWORTH, Sir William: ?-1385
Killed Wat Tylor

Originally St Michael's, Crooked
Lane, London D. Reburied in yard
of St Martin Orgar, London

WATT, James: 1736-1819
Improver of the steam engine

St Mary's, Handsworth, Warwicks,
MEM WA North Choir Aisle

WATTS, George Frederick: 1817-1904
Artist, sculptor

Watts Cemetery Chapel, Compton,
Surrey YD

WATTS, Isaac: 1674-1748
Hymn writer

Bunhill Fields, London T.
MEM WA South Choir Aisle

WAUGH, Evelyn: 1903-1966
Novelist

St Peter and St Paul's,
Combe Florry, Somerset YD

WEBB, Beatrice: 1858-1943
Baroness Passfield, social reformer

Originally Passfield, Suffolk,
moved to WA Nave

WEBB, Sidney: 1859-1947
Baron Passfield, social reformer

Originally Passfield, Suffolk,
moved to WA Nave

WEDGWOOD, Josiah: 1730-1795
Potter

St Peter-ad-Vincula, Stoke-on-
Trent, Staffs

WEEVER, John: 1576-1632
Author of 'Ancient Funeral Monuments'

St Mary's, Finsbury, London D

WELLINGTON, Arthur Wellesley: 1769-1852
1st Duke of, soldier & statesman

St Paul's Cathedral, London T

Copenhagen: 1808-1836
The horse Wellington rode at Waterloo

Stratfield Saye, Hants

WELLS, H G: 1866-1946
(Herbert George) Novelist

Ashes in sea, Isle of Wight

WENTWORTH, Thomas
See **Strafford**

WESLEY, Charles: 1707-1788
18th child, brother of John, evangelist

Old Marylebone, London YD D
MEM WA South Choir Aisle

WESLEY, John: 1703-1791
15th child, founder of Methodism

City Road Chapel, London T
MEM WA South Choir Aisle

WESLEY, Mary: 1696-1781
Wife of John

St Giles, Camberwell, London D

WESLEY, Samuel: 1662-1735
Father of John & 18 other children

St Andrew, Epworth, Lincs YD G

WESLEY, Susannah: 1669-1742
Mother of John and 18 other children

Bunhill Fields, London

WEST, Benjamin: 1738-1820
Artist

St Paul's Cathedral, London

WEST, Thomas: 1472-1554
9th Baron de la Warr. With Henry VIII
at Field of Cloth of Gold

St Mary's Broadwater, West Sussex
T. Chantry chapel Boxgrove,
West Sussex

WESTMACOTT, Sir Richard: 1775-1856
Sculptor

St Mary's, Chastleton, Oxon, YD

WHISTLER, James Abbott McNeill: 1834-1903
American painter

St Nicholas, Chiswick, London YD
T with wife and mother

WHITBREAD, Samuel: 1720-1796
Brewer, philanthropist

St Mary, Cardington, Beds T

WHITE (or WITE or CANDIDA): ?-900
Except for Edward the Confessor,
the only English Saint whose remains
are still in their original tomb

St Candida and Holy Cross,
Whitchurch Canonicorum,
Dorset T

WHITE, Gilbert: 1720-1793
Naturalist

St Mary's, Selbourne, Hants YD G

WHITTINGTON, Dick: c1358-1423
Sir Richard, Lord Mayor of London
4 times, cat unknown until 1605

St Michael Paternoster Royal,
London D

WILBERFORCE, William: 1759-1833
Anti-slavery

WA North Transept
MON WA North Choir Aisle

WILDE, Oscar: 1854-1900
Writer

Originally in Bagneaux Cemetery,
removed 1909 to Père Lachaise,
Paris, MON. MEM WA Poets'
Corner window

WILSON, Harold: 1916-1995
Baron Wilson of Rievaulx
PM 1964-1970 & 1974-1976

Old Church, St Mary's, Isles of
Scilly YD

WOLFE, General James: 1727-1759
Soldier, captured Quebec

St Alfege's, Greenwich
MEM WA North Ambulatory

WOLSEY, Cardinal Thomas: 1475-1530
Prelate and statesman

St Mary de Pratis Abbey,
Leicester D

WOOD, Sir Henry: 1869-1944
Founder of Promenade Concerts

Holy Sepulchre, Holborn Viaduct,
London

WOODFORDE-FINDEN, Amy: 1860-1919
Composer, 'India Love Lyrics'

St Thomas Becket, Hampsthwaite,
Yorkshire

WOODWARD, Dr John: 1665-1728
Geologist, natural historian

WA Nave

WOOLF, Virginia: 1882-1941
Novelist

Garden of Monk's House,
Rodmell, East Sussex

WORDSWORTH, William: 1770-1850
Poet Laureate

St Oswald, Grasmere, Cumbria,
YD, with daughter Dorothy and
sister Dorothy Statue WA Poets'
Corner

WOTTON, Sir Henry: 1568-1639
Provost of Eton

Eton College Chapel

WREN, Sir Christopher: 1632-1723
Architect

St Paul's Cathedral, London G

WRIOTHESLEY, Sir Thomas: 1505-1550
1st Earl of Southampton, statesman

Originally St Andrew's, Holborn,
London. Re-interred St Peter's
Titchfield, Hants T

WROTH, William: 1576-1652
Founded first Welsh non-conformist chapel,
'Blessed Apostle South Wales'

St Dyfrig, Llanvaches, Gwent

WYATT, James: 1746-1813
Architect, his restoration work on cathedrals
earned him the title 'The Great Destroyer'

WA Poets' Corner

WYATT, Sir Thomas: 1503-1452
Poet

Sherborne Minster, Dorset

WYATTVILLE, Sir Jeffrey: 1766-1840
Architect, nephew of James Wyatt

St George's Chapel, Windsor

WYCHERLEY, William: 1640-1716
Dramatist

St Paul's, Covent Garden, London

WYCLIFEE, John: 1329-1384
Religious reformer, writings condemned

St Mary, Lutterworth, Leicester D.
Body burned, ashes thrown in
river in 1428

YALE, Elihu: 1649-1721
US university named after him

St Giles, Wrexham, Clwyd Wales T

YEATS, W B: 1865-1939
(William Butler) Poet

Originally Roquebrune, France,
removed 1948 to Protestant
churchyard, Drumcliff, Sligo,
Ireland

YELVERTON, Sir Christopher: 1535-1612
1st Lord Chief Justice to Elizabeth

St Peter and St Paul, Easton
Maudit, Northants T

YEVELE, Henry: ?-1400
Architect west end of WA, also Westminster
Hall & designer of tombs of Richard II
and Edward III

St Magnus the Martyr, London D

ZOFFANY, John: 1733-1810
Artist

St Anne's, Kew Green, London

OTHER TITLES AVAILABLE

HISTORY

The Death of Kings –
How the Kings and Queens of England died

LITERARY QUIZ & PUZZLE BOOK

Bronte Sisters
Charles Dickens
Gilbert & Sullivan
Jane Austen
Shakespeare
Sherlock Holmes
Thomas Hardy

SLANG AND DIALECT GLOSSARIES

American English/English American
Australian English/English Australian
Cumbrian English
Gay Slang
Geordie English
Irish English/English Irish
Hip Hop English
Home Counties English
Lancashire English
London Taxi Driver Slang
Military Slang
Playground Slang
Police Slang
Prison Slang
Rhyming Cockney Slang
Rude Rhyming Slang
Scottish English/English Scottish
Scouse English
West Country English
Yiddish English/English Yiddish
Yorkshire English

All of these titles area available from good
booksellers or by contacting the publisher:
Abson Books London
5 Sidney Square London E1 2EY
Tel 020 7790 4737 Fax 020 7790 7346
email absonbooks@aol.com
web www.absonbooks.co.uk